THE LITTLE GUI

PIZZAS

THE LITTLE GUIDES

PIZZAS

Published by Fog City Press
814 Montgomery Street
San Francisco, CA 94133 USA
Reprinted in 2000 (twice), 2001 (twice), 2002 (twice), 2003

Chief Executive Officer: John Owen
President: Terry Newell
Publisher: Lynn Humphries
Managing Editor: Janine Flew
Coordinating Designer: Helen Perks
Editorial Coordinator: Kiren Thandi
Production Manager: Caroline Webber
Production Coordinator: James Blackman
Sales Manager: Emily Jahn
Vice President International Sales: Stuart Laurence

Project Editor: Narelle Walford
Designer: Katie Ravich

A catalog record for this book is available from
the Library of Congress, Washington, DC.

ISBN 1 875137 78 5

Color reproduction by Colourscan Co Pte Ltd
Printed by LeeFung-Asco Printers
Printed in China

A Weldon Owen Production

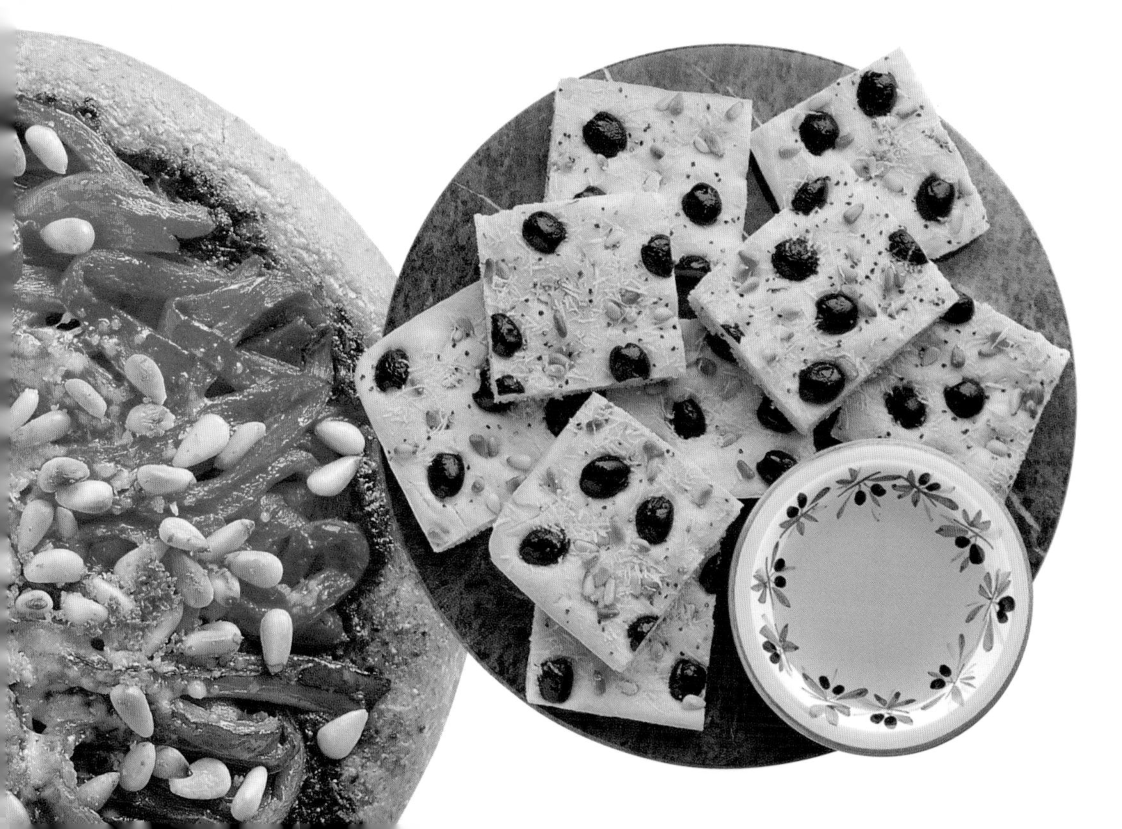

CONTENTS

PART ONE

THE BASICS

PART TWO

RECIPES

Introduction

Most associated with the enjoyment of eating pizza is the experience of the pizzeria.

The aroma usually grabs you before you ever set eyes on a pizzeria. The air becomes filled with the scent of tomatoes, garlic, herbs, baking bread and bubbling cheese. Irresistibly, you are drawn to the source.

Inside, you encounter the convivial hum of contented diners and furnishings that are simple and spare, almost ascetic. The food, the sights, the sounds, the aromas all make you feel comfortably at home, among family. This is what brings you back, again and again, to a great pizzeria.

A meal at a pizzeria is slice-of-life theater. Star of the show is the *pizzaiolo,* or pizza maker. Always onstage at the oven, the *pizzaiolo* performs acts of culinary conjuring.

Surrounding him are containers holding all the colors, textures, tastes and scents that will give character to his creations: ripe red plum tomatoes; mounds of fresh mozzarella; lustrous dark olives; silvery anchovy fillets; bouquets of basil and oregano; salt-encrusted capers; freshly ground black peppercorns and red chilies. The *pizzaiolo* goes to work, often sending a round of dough whirling off his fists into the air as he stretches it out to the ideal dimensions. And you look on, fascinated by this now-signature feat of pizza making.

With a little magic, you can bring the flavor of the pizzeria home. Special pizza-making equipment can help you achieve authentic results. Intense heat and direct contact of the dough with the heat source are crucial to create a great pizza, with a well-crisped crust that finishes baking in the same time it takes the topping to cook.

Pizza bricks or tiles transform a home oven into an environment that resembles a traditional bread oven. Follow the manufacturer's directions and allow them to preheat while the oven does. Easiest to find, and most readily adaptable to gas and electric ovens, are round pizza bricks that are placed on an oven rack set at the lowest level. Or you can cook your pizza on a baking sheet.

Next, a pizza peel, a wide wooden spatula with a long handle, makes sliding a pizza into the oven a safe and simple task. If you prefer not to invest in a peel, you can use an inverted rimless baking sheet.

Many of the topping ingredients for pizza can be prepared ahead of time and assembled just before cooking. Also, all pizza doughs can be made in advance and stored in the refrigerator or freezer.

U.S. cup measures are used throughout this book. Slight adjustments may need to be made to quantities if Imperial or Metric cups are used.

PART ONE

THE BASICS

Whether the canvas of a painting, the foundations of a new home or the base of a pizza, the success of any finished product depends upon quality groundwork. Begin to create both the character and flavor of your pizza with the type of dough and sauce you choose.

DOUGHS

Types of Doughs

Many of the types of bread now eaten in Italy were first made in ancient times. Among them are the larger loaves that are prepared at home in certain towns in Apulia and Basilicata, and taken to the village oven to bake, each identified by a wooden stamp used by the family to imprint their initials or a rustic design on the dough.

Of ancient origin, too, are the Sicilian breads enriched with saffron and sesame seeds similar to those made in Asia Minor and along the North African Mediterranean coast. The paper-thin Sardinian *carta da musica* (music paper) and the *piadina* of Romagna are both similar to the unleavened matzoh the Jewish people eat once a year to commemorate the journey of the chosen people across the Red Sea.

It is a very short step from bread to pizza, not least because no pizza can be made without using bread dough as a start.

Pizza is an ancient food, born of the need to find a simple way of enriching bread to make it tastier and more substantial. The oldest example is a plain pizza the Neapolitans call *alla Mastu Nicola*, probably in honor of a pizza-maker by the name of Nicola who made it famous. The circle of dough is spread with a little pork fat and topped with slices of cheese, some salt and pepper and basil leaves.

The pizza is an ideal example of dietary balance: a little flour, water, a pinch of yeast, oil, tomato and cheese, all blended perfectly together through rapid cooking. The universal success of the pizza is contained within this simple formula, and in the many transformations that are accomplished by simply adding or replacing one or more components. The variations are endless. Spread your ingredients over a circle of rolled-out dough, and you have a pizza. Gather the ingredients in the center of the dough and fold it in half and you have a calzone, which can be either baked or fried.

Focaccia (meaning "cake" or "bun") is similar to pizza in that they are both flat breads topped with various savory ingredients. Focaccia is usually more simply topped, perhaps with just a little olive oil, herbs, onions or olives.

Pizza lovers can be very fussy when it comes to just what they think makes a good pizza base. Gathered here is a selection of pizzas bases for you to try. The pizzas included in the Recipes section of this book specifically utilize one of these delicious bases. Take a look; you may be surprised that such a plain element of a pizza can actually be a whole new adventure.

The various doughs require different kinds of handling according to the ingredients used. Some, such as wholewheat, can simply be pressed out with your fingers. Neapolitan pizza dough, on the other hand, is more elastic and needs to be gently stretched and twirled until it is the right size and thickness. Instructions are given in each recipe for which method to follow.

Varying the pizza base, from the basic pizza dough through to focaccia, tortilla, semolina, Neapolitan, cornmeal, wholewheat and yeast-free pizza doughs and sourdough, will add to the taste sensations of your pizza creations.

STEPS FOR MAKING YEAST-RISEN PIZZA DOUGH

Dry active yeast begins to work as soon as it is wet. So be sure to keep it perfectly dry until you're ready to use it.

STEP 1

Prepare Yeast

Combine 2 teaspoons active dry yeast, 1 teaspoon sugar, 1/2 teaspoon salt, 1 tablespoon olive oil and 1/2 cup/ 4 fl oz/125 ml water in a bowl. Set aside for around 10 minutes, or until frothy.

If your yeast hasn't foamed and bubbled, it won't raise the dough, so start again with new yeast.

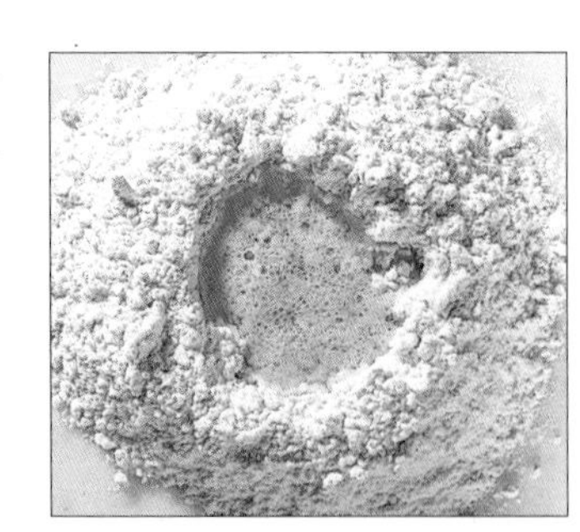

STEP 2

Add Flour

Place 1 1/2 cups/6 oz/185 g all-purpose (plain) flour on a pastry slab or in a large bowl. Make a well in the center and add the yeast mixture.

It is the gluten protein in the yeast that makes the dough strong and elastic.

STEP 3

Combine

Combine by gradually incorporating the flour into the yeast mixture, adding a little extra water if necessary. (Alternatively, combine the mixture in a food processor.)

Kneading the dough helps to evenly distribute the yeast and gives the dough a smooth texture.

STEP 4

Knead

Transfer the dough to a floured board and knead until it is smooth and elastic, about 5 minutes. Place the dough in a large, lightly oiled bowl. Cover and place in a warm, draft-free place for 30 minutes or until doubled in size.

Makes one 12-in/30-cm pizza base
Preparation time 50 minutes

Focaccia Pizza Dough

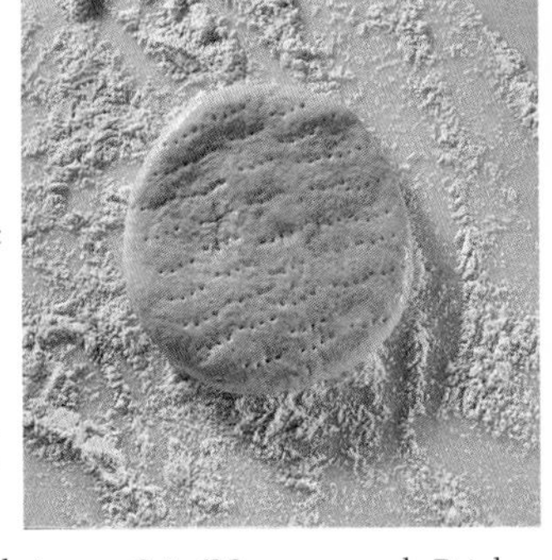

Combine 2 cups/8 oz/250 g of all-purpose (plain) flour with 1 tablespoon active dry yeast, 1¼ cups/10 fl oz/300 ml water and 1 teaspoon sea salt in a bowl. Beat until well mixed, cover and set aside in a warm place until it has doubled in size, about 20 minutes.

Place 1½ cups/6 oz/185 g of flour and 4 tablespoons/2 oz/60 g butter on a board. Spoon the risen yeast mixture into the center of the flour and gradually combine until all of the flour is incorporated. Knead until smooth and elastic, about 5 minutes.

Divide the dough into three equal portions. Press each portion of dough into a 9-in/22-cm round. Prick well with a fork. Place each round on an oiled baking sheet.
Brush the tops with olive oil.

Set the focaccia dough aside in a warm, draft-free place until it has doubled in size, about 40 minutes. Meanwhile, preheat oven to 425°F/210°C/Gas Mark 5.

Bake until golden brown on top, about 25 minutes. Cool on a rack. The extra focaccias can be frozen before or after baking. If preparing the dough in advance, extend the proofing time of the dough by placing it in the refrigerator.

Makes three 9-in/22-cm focaccias
Preparation/Cooking time 1 hour 40 minutes

Tortilla Pizza Dough

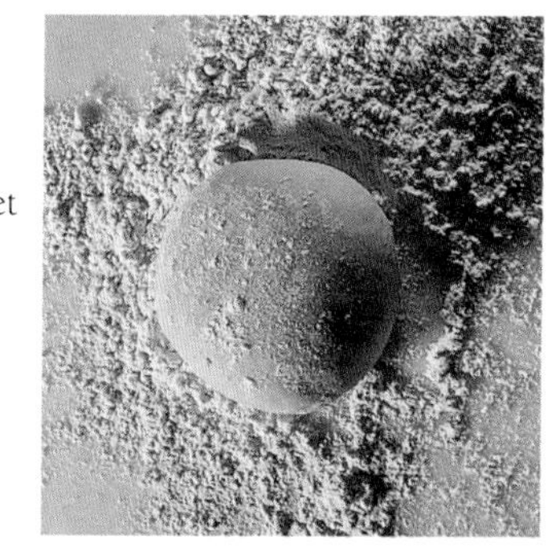

Place 1/2 cup/2 oz/60 g all-purpose (plain) flour, 1 cup/4 oz/125 g tortilla flour (masa harina) or extra-fine cornmeal (maize flour) or millet meal, 2 teaspoons baking powder and 1/2 teaspoon of salt in a bowl. Make a well in the center and add 1/3 cup/2 1/2 fl oz/80 ml water and 2 tablespoons olive oil.

Proceed as for Yeast-Risen Dough. Once kneaded, it is ready to use.

Makes one 12-in/30-cm pizza base
Preparation time 15 minutes

Semolina Pizza Dough

Place 1/2 cup/2 oz/60 g semolina flour, 1 cup/4 oz/125 g all-purpose (plain) flour,* 2 teaspoons baking powder and 1/2 teaspoon salt in a bowl. Make a well in the center and add 1/2 cup/4 fl oz/ 125 ml water and 2 tablespoons olive oil.

Proceed as for Yeast-Risen Dough. Once kneaded, it is ready to use.

Makes one 12-inch (30-cm) pizza base **Preparation time** 15 minutes
***Self-rising flour can be used** instead of all-purpose flour and baking powder.

Yeast-Free Pizza Dough

Place 1½ cups/6 oz/185 g all-purpose (plain) flour,* 1 tablespoon baki powder and ½ teaspoon salt in a bowl. Make a well in the center and ad ½ cup/4 fl oz/125 ml water and 2 tablespoons olive oil.

Proceed as for Yeast-Risen Dough. Once kneaded, it is ready to use.

Makes one 12-in/30-cm pizza base **Preparation time** 15 minutes
***Self-rising flour can be used** instead of all-purpose flour and baking powder.

Sourdough Pizza Dough

To make the starter: Combine 1 teaspoon active dry yeast and 1 cup/ 8 fl oz/250 ml water. Whisk in 1 cup/4 oz/125 g all-purpose (plain) flour. Cover with plastic wrap and set aside at room temperature for 3 to 24 hours, until frothy. (The longer the souring time, the sourer the dough.) Add ½ teaspoon of salt and 2 cups/8 oz/250 g all-purpose (plain) flour to the starter. Knead until pliable, about 5 minutes. Set aside in a warm place until it has nearly doubled in size, about 40 minutes.

Makes one 9-in/22-cm sourdough base
Preparation time 4–25 hours

Cornmeal Pizza Dough

Place 1/2 cup/2 1/2 oz/75 g yellow cornmeal (maize flour) or polenta, 1 cup/4 oz/125 g all-purpose (plain) flour,* 2 teaspoons baking powder and 1/2 teaspoon salt in a bowl. Make a well in the center and add 1/2 cup/4 fl oz/125 ml water and 2 tablespoons olive oil.

Proceed as for Yeast-Risen Dough. Once kneaded, it is ready to use.

Makes one 12-in/30-cm pizza base **Preparation time** 15 minutes
*__Self-rising flour can be used__ instead of all-purpose flour and baking powder.

Wholewheat Pizza Dough

Place 1 1/2 cups/7 oz/220 g wholewheat flour, 1 tablespoon baking powder and 1/2 teaspoon salt in a bowl. Make a well in the center and add 1/2 cup plus 2 tablespoons/5 fl oz/160ml water and 2 tablespoons olive oil.

Proceed as for Yeast-Risen Dough. Once kneaded, it is ready to use.

Makes one 12-in/30-cm pizza base
Preparation time 15 minutes

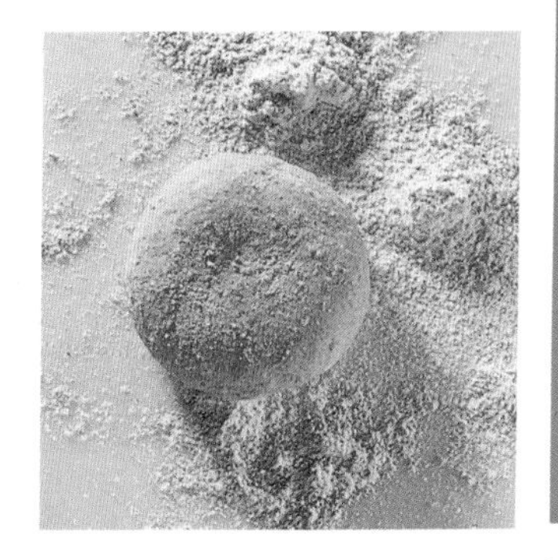

Neapolitan Pizza Dough

A Neapolitan pizza crust must be thin, but not cracker-thin as is traditional in Rome. If you prefer an extra-crisp super-thin crust, roll the dough into a round 11 in/28 cm in diameter rather than the 9 in/22 cm specified in the pizza recipes. Note that these directions make enough for two crusts. All the pizza recipes in this book that use this dough call for only half that amount. You can refrigerate the extra dough for up to two days or freeze for up to one month, or double the topping ingredients and make two pizzas.

INGREDIENTS

1½ teaspoons active dry yeast

¼ cup/2 fl oz/60 ml lukewarm water (105°F/42°C)

1½ tablespoons olive oil

½ cup/4 fl oz/125 ml cold water

1⅔ cups/7 oz/200 g unbleached all-purpose (plain) flour, plus extra for kneading

¾ teaspoon salt

METHOD FOR MAKING NEAPOLITAN PIZZA DOUGH

In a large mixing bowl, stir the yeast into the lukewarm water. Let stand until creamy, about 10 minutes. Stir in the olive oil and the cold water, and then whisk in ½ cup/2 oz/60 g of the flour and the salt, stirring until smooth. Stir in the remaining flour, ½ cup/2 oz/60 g at a time, until the dough comes together in a rough mass.

On a lightly floured work surface, knead the dough until smooth and velvety, 8–10 minutes. It will be soft. Cover loosely with a kitchen towel and let rest for 15 minutes.

Divide into two equal portions, knead briefly, then roll each portion into a smooth, tight round ball. To use the dough immediately, sprinkle a little flour on the work surface and set the balls on it. Cover them with a kitchen towel and let rise for 1 hour, then stretch and top the dough as directed in each recipe.

This delicious Pizza with Yellow Bell Peppers and Capers (page 83) uses Neapolitan pizza dough for its base.

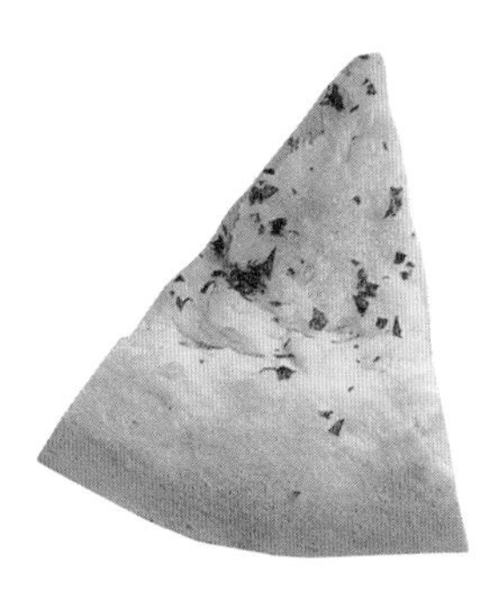

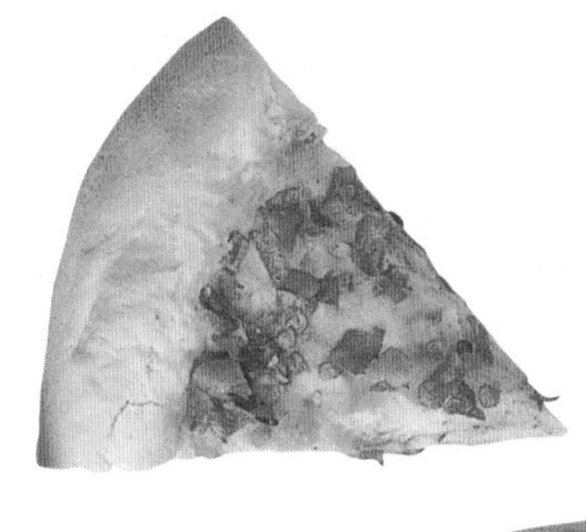

Neapolitan's crispy crust is perfect for a variety of simple toppings.

You may also store one or both balls of dough until ready to use. For short-term storage and for a slow rise resulting in more flavor, place the dough balls on a small baking pan lined with a kitchen towel, cover them with a second towel and refrigerate for up to 48 hours; remove from the refrigerator and let stand at room temperature for 10–15 minutes before forming the pizza. For longer storage, slip each flour-dusted ball into a plastic freezer bag, seal tightly and freeze for up to 1 month. Before use, place the frozen dough in a lightly oiled bowl, cover loosely with plastic wrap, and let thaw overnight in the refrigerator or for about 2 hours at room temperature. The thawed dough should be puffy and soft to the touch.

Makes enough for two 9-in/22-cm pizza bases **Preparation time** 1 hour and 45 minutes

Herb-Flavored Focaccia

Focaccia dough is softer than pizza dough, yielding a nearly cakelike interior once it is baked. Baking the focaccia in 8-in/20-cm cake pans results in rounds 1½ in/4 cm thick—perfect for pairing with an unlimited variety of panino fillings or slicing to serve plain as an accompaniment to any meal. If you prefer a crisp crust, drizzle the dough with a generous amount of olive oil before baking. For a soft crust, brush the focaccia with olive oil immediately upon removing it from the oven.

INGREDIENTS

2½ teaspoons (1 package) active dry yeast

1 cup/8 fl oz/250 ml lukewarm water (105°F/42°C)

2 tablespoons olive oil

2 cups/8 oz/250 g unbleached all-purpose (plain) flour, plus extra for kneading

1 teaspoon salt

2 tablespoons chopped fresh chives

1 tablespoon chopped fresh thyme

1½ teaspoons finely chopped fresh rosemary

Extra-virgin olive oil for brushing

Coarse salt

Popular all over Italy, this rustic flat bread of Etruscan origin predates the Neapolitan pizza by centuries. A special section on focaccia and panini begins on page 194. The one pictured here is Focaccia with Coarse Salt (page 202).

METHOD FOR MAKING HERB-FLAVORED FOCACCIA

In a large mixing bowl, stir the yeast into ¼ cup/2 fl oz/60 ml of the lukewarm water. Let stand until creamy, about 10 minutes. Stir in the remaining ¾ cup/6 fl oz/190 ml lukewarm water and the olive oil. Add 1 cup/4 oz/125 g of the flour and the salt and whisk until smooth. Add the chives, thyme and rosemary and mix well, then stir in the remaining 1 cup/4 oz/125 g flour, ½ cup/2 oz/60 g at a time, until the dough comes together in a rough mass.

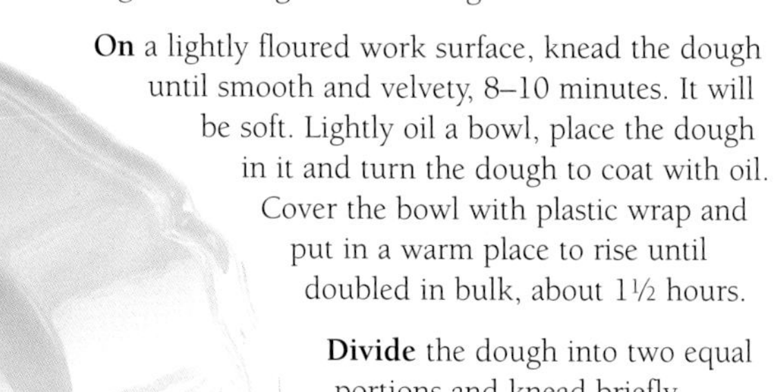

On a lightly floured work surface, knead the dough until smooth and velvety, 8–10 minutes. It will be soft. Lightly oil a bowl, place the dough in it and turn the dough to coat with oil. Cover the bowl with plastic wrap and put in a warm place to rise until doubled in bulk, about 1½ hours.

Divide the dough into two equal portions and knead briefly. The dough is now ready to be stretched and topped as directed

The recipe for this tasty panino, or Eggplant, Tomato and Mozzarella Sandwich, can be found on page 232.

in the recipes or baked plain as directed below. You may also store the dough, as directed for the Neapolitan Pizza Dough (*page* 22), until ready to use. If you prefer thinner, more resilient focaccia, stretch out the dough into a larger pan.

If plain focaccia is preferred, lightly oil two 8-in/20-cm cake pans. Place each portion of dough in a prepared pan and gently stretch it out to the edges, pulling it from the center outward to achieve an even thickness. If the dough springs back toward the center and is difficult to work with, cover and set it aside for 10 minutes to relax, then continue coaxing the dough out to an even thickness. Cover the pans with kitchen towels and let dough rise until almost doubled in bulk and very soft and puffy, about 45 minutes.

Preheat an oven to 475°F/230°C/Gas Mark 6. Using your fingertips, dimple the dough in several places, leaving indentations about ½ in/13 mm deep. Again cover the pans with towels and let rise for another 20 minutes.

Bake until golden brown and cooked through, 15–18 minutes. Remove from the oven and immediately brush the tops with a generous amount of extra-virgin olive oil, then sprinkle with coarse salt. Serve hot or at room temperature.

Makes two 8-in/20-cm rounds **Preparation time** just over 2 hours

SAUCES

Types of Sauces

Pizza creation is a layer-by-layer experience. Having chosen the base, the next task is to find just the right sauce to cover it—one that will complement both the flavor and texture of the base as well as the various toppings you have chosen for your pizza.

The best-known and best-loved pizza sauce is a simple tomato sauce. The tomato was one of the ingredients of the first pizza, the Neapolitan.

Originating in South America, the tomato was considered poisonous by many in Europe from its arrival there in the mid-fifteenth century. As a result, the tomato did not become widely accepted throughout Europe as a food until the early 1800s.

However, by that time the Italians had begun cultivating it, and the tomato remains an essential ingredient of the cuisine of Italy. Across Europe, the tomato gained in reputation and in the nineteenth century was already the second most popularly consumed vegetable of most western countries (the first being the potato).

As the pizza has continued to evolve over the centuries, so too has the variety of delectable sauces that can be utilized. Basic tomato sauce has a simple and lovely rich flavor, but isn't the full spectrum you can choose from. Included in this section are recipes for Spicy Tomato Sauce, Sun-Dried Tomato Sauce, Uncooked Tomato Sauce and Tomato–Basil Sauce.

And then there's the well-loved Pesto, including Genovese Pesto, just for something different. Made with quintessentially Italian ingredients—basil, olive oil, and Parmesan cheese—pesto sits as comfortably on a pizza as the more traditional tomato sauce.

Pesto (opposite) reveals Italian cuisine's success in its simple combinations of fresh ingredients.

Basic Tomato Sauce

INGREDIENTS

2 large onions

2 cloves garlic

1 tablespoon olive oil

2 lb/1 kg ripe tomatoes

Canned tomatoes possess similar nutritional content to fresh ones—just watch the added salt.

STEP 1

Prepare

Peel and finely chop the onions and garlic. Sauté in the olive oil over low heat for approximately 10 minutes, or until they are transparent. Roughly chop the tomatoes and add to the onions.

A pizza's bubbling sauce, as well as its baking dough, brings an inviting savory aroma to your kitchen.

STEP 2

Cook

Cook the mixture over a medium heat for 35–40 minutes, or until it begins to thicken. Cool.

This lovely and thick sauce is the perfect choice when you need a simple base that will work with a wide variety of pizza toppings.

STEP 3

Store

This mixture can be stored in the refrigerator for up to one week.

Makes 4 cups/32 fl oz/1 l
Preparation/Cooking time 50 minutes

Sun-Dried Tomato Sauce

Drain and purée $9\frac{1}{2}$ oz/300 g sun-dried tomatoes in olive oil. Add the purée, plus 1 tablespoon finely chopped basil leaves, to 1 quantity of Basic Tomato Sauce (*page 34*).

Spicy Tomato Sauce

Finely chop 1–2 fresh red or green chilies, or to taste, and add to the onions when making 1 quantity of Basic Tomato Sauce (*page 34*).

Spicy Tomato Sauce adds even more zing to this Herb Pizza's rich assortment of flavors. The recipe for this highly aromatic pizza can be found on page 80.

Uncooked Tomato Sauce

This simple sauce is the traditional topping on a Neapolitan pizza and suits a wide range of pizza preparations. It is light on the palate and fulfills its role as an undernote to pizza, allowing the additional toppings to stand out. If you are using canned tomatoes, look for the sweetest ones you can find. Taste them and, if they are a bit too acidic, add a pinch of sugar.

INGREDIENTS

8 ripe plum (Roma) tomatoes or
1 small can/16 oz/500 g plum (Roma) tomatoes with their juices

1 tablespoon extra-virgin olive oil

Salt and freshly ground pepper

Fit a food mill with the coarse or medium blade and place over a small mixing bowl. Peel the fresh tomatoes, if using. Pass the tomatoes through the mill into the bowl. Alternatively, use a food processor. Place the fresh or canned tomatoes in a food processor fitted with the metal blade and pulse to form a coarse purée. Add the olive oil and season to taste with salt and pepper. Use immediately, or transfer to a tightly covered container and refrigerate for up to two days.

Makes about 1½ cups/12 fl oz/375 ml, enough for six 9-in/22-cm pizzas **Preparation time** 10 minutes

Tomato–Basil Sauce

This flavorful, yet basic, sauce embodies the simple, rustic elegance of classic Italian cooking at its best. It is used in a wide range of Italian dishes, including soups, pastas, baked dishes, risotto and, of course, pizzas, to which it adds a deeper, more fully developed flavor than the uncooked tomato sauce on the previous page. If you find that your tomatoes lack a good balance of sweetness and acidity, add a few pinches of sugar to bring out their natural sweetness.

INGREDIENTS

1/4 cup/2 fl oz/60 ml extra-virgin olive oil

2 cloves garlic, minced

12 plum (Roma) tomatoes, peeled, seeded and chopped, or 1 large can/28 oz/875 g plum (Roma) tomatoes, chopped, with their juices

8 large fresh basil leaves, coarsely chopped

Salt and freshly ground pepper

METHOD FOR MAKING TOMATO–BASIL SAUCE

In a large frying pan over medium heat, warm the extra-virgin olive oil. Add the garlic and sauté for a few seconds just until fragrant. Add the tomatoes and cook, stirring frequently, until they begin to break down and form a sauce, about 10 minutes.

Add the basil, season to taste with salt and pepper and raise the heat to medium-high. Cook, stirring occasionally, until the sauce thickens and is no longer watery, 15–20 minutes.

Use immediately, or transfer to a container with a tight-fitting lid and refrigerate for up to two days.

Makes about 2 cups/16 fl oz/500 ml
Preparation/Cooking time 35 minutes

Pizza Margherita allows you to savor a slice of Italian culture and history. The recipe for this Neapolitan delight (on page 65) utilizes Tomato–Basil Sauce.

Genovese Pesto

Few sauces represent a season as perfectly as this summer sauce from Liguria. The distinct flavors of basil and garlic, mellowed with Italian Parmesan, give it a versatility matched by few other sauces. It can be used for pasta and pizza, spread on crostini and panini, even used as a marinade for roasted meats. Vary the amount of olive oil according to your own preferences: use less for a light, fluffy texture and more for a denser, heavier and more flavorful sauce.

INGREDIENTS

1/4 cup/1 oz/30 g pine nuts or walnuts

2 cups/2 oz/60 g firmly packed fresh basil leaves

4–6 cloves garlic

1/2–1 cup/4–8 fl oz/125–250 ml extra-virgin olive oil

1/4 cup/1 oz/30 g freshly grated Italian Parmesan cheese

1/4 cup/1 oz/30 g freshly grated Italian pecorino romano cheese

Salt and freshly ground pepper

METHOD FOR MAKING GENOVESE PESTO

Preheat an oven to 350°F/180°C/Gas Mark 4. Spread the nuts in a single layer on a baking sheet. Place in the oven until lightly toasted and fragrant, about 8 minutes. (If using pine nuts, watch them carefully as they burn very quickly.) Remove from the heat and allow to cool.

In a food processor fitted with the metal blade or in a blender, combine the basil and garlic and pulse until finely chopped, scraping down the sides of the bowl as necessary. With the motor running, add ½ cup/4 fl oz/125 ml of the olive oil in a slow, steady stream. Scatter the cheeses over the top, then pulse until the cheeses are absorbed. Again with the motor running, slowly add the remaining oil and process until creamy.

Season to taste with salt and pepper, add the nuts and pulse just until the nuts are coarsely chopped. Use immediately, or pour into a container and top with a thin layer of olive oil. Cover tightly and refrigerate for up to four days.

Makes about 2 cups/16 fl oz/500 ml
Preparation/Cooking time 20 minutes

This quintessential Italian combination of basil, olive oil and Parmesan cheese is most delicious when homemade. Genovese Pesto is the best known of them all.

Pesto

INGREDIENTS

1 large bunch fresh basil, stems removed, leaves washed and dried

1/4 cup/3/4 oz/25g pine nuts

1/2 cup/1 3/4 oz/50g grated Parmesan cheese

2 cloves garlic, peeled

1/2 cup/4 fl oz/125 ml olive oil

STEPS FOR MAKING PESTO

STEP 1

Blend
Combine the basil leaves, pine nuts, Parmesan and the garlic cloves in a food processor or blender. Blend until smooth.

STEP 2

Add Oil
Add the oil very gradually, processing until the mixture is well combined.

STEP 3

Store
Store in the refrigerator topped with a film of oil (to prevent discoloration) until required. Any excess pesto may be frozen.

Makes 1½ cups/12 fl oz/375 ml **Preparation/Cooking time** 10 minutes

GIURLANI

PART TWO

RECIPES

This section reveals the true versatility of pizza. Whether you're looking for traditional or modern Italian styles or exotic adaptations from other countries, here you'll find the the perfect pizza snack, meal or dessert.

HISTORY OF PIZZA

History of Pizza

The roots of the modern pizza may be traced back to the first century AD, when the ancient Greeks, who occupied southern Italy for centuries, baked disks of risen bread dough in hot ovens to create edible plates soaked with drippings and seasonings from the main course. This practice led to topping the dough with seasonings before it went into the oven, yielding the oldest known ancestor of the legendary Neapolitan pizza.

But it wasn't until some time after the tomato arrived in Naples from the New World in the sixteenth century that pizzas even began to resemble the food that people all over the world know and love so well today.

Ingenious Neapolitans changed pizzas forever with the addition of the *pomodoro* (tomato), a food that Italians once believed to be poisonous. This succulent fruit became the staple topping for most pizzas, a fact that was immortalized and given the royal seal of approval—and resulted in a humble pizza being named after a queen.

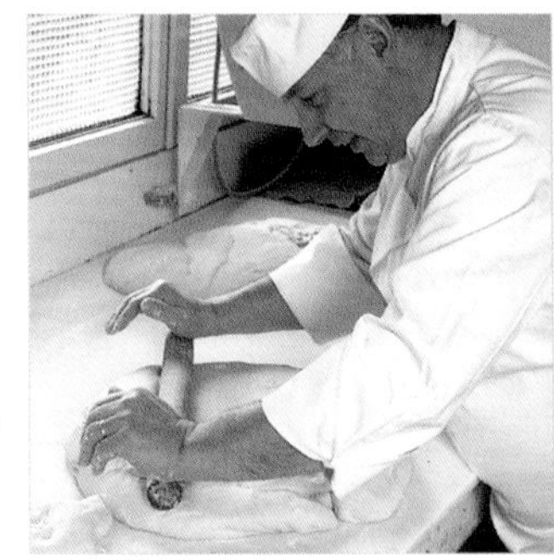

The Pizza Margherita was named after Queen Margherita of Savoie, who tasted this variety of pizza during a visit to Naples in 1889 and declared it was her favorite. It is made with a handful of basil leaves, tomato and mozzarella cheese, ingredients that possessed the three colors of the Italian flag—red, white and green.

Tomatoes and mozzarella cheese made from buffalo milk were two of the region's best products. Classic Neapolitan pizza includes these products, as well as oregano and anchovies.

Soon after tomatoes joined the dough, the modern pizzeria had its humble beginnings in the streets of Naples as a way to provide quick, basic food—literally, the daily bread—to hungry Neapolitan working people. Small rooms were cut into the city's venerable stone walls to house beehive-shaped ovens in which *pizzaioli*, or "pizza makers," would bake disks of dough, topped simply with tomatoes, a drizzle of olive oil and some oregano.

Hot from the oven, the pizzas would be folded in half, tucked into a sheet from yesterday's newspaper and sold over the counter to be eaten in the street. Nineteenth-century travelers in Italy described the street vendors who walked the city's narrow streets calling to the citizens to come and buy their tasty pizzas. Customers would purchase a piece (at a discount if it were cold), fold it in half and eat these *libretti* ("little books") while they took their stroll around town or continued on longer journeys.

The late nineteenth and early twentieth centuries saw many workers leave Naples in search of better lives in America, and the *pizzaioli* brought their talent and recipes with them.

Italian immigrants began their American careers working in Italian bakeries, where pizza first appeared as focaccia, or "pan pizza", with a thicker, more breadlike crust resembling pizzas of the south. In Little Italy in New York, a now famous Neapolitan, Gennaro Lombardi, opened the first pizzeria in 1895.

Upon saving a bit of money, these new immigrants opened their own pizza shops, offering over-the-counter service like their ancestors in the old country. Pizzerias continued to follow in the path of Italian migration to the New World and later to other parts of Europe.

Unfortunately, the pizza lost much of its authentic flavor along the way. But in its home town, if you are lucky enough to find a traditional pizzeria with an expert *pizzaiolo*, you can sample the original kind of pizza: a humble yet delicious dish with lively, direct flavors.

The Great Depression of the 1930s saw many pizzerias open, providing reasonably priced sustenance to struggling families. But it was with the return of the GIs from Europe after World War II that pizza began to develop the extra-ordinary following it has today.

As pizzerias gained in popularity in the late 1950s and early 1960s, they grew in size, adding tables and amplifying the menu with simple regional Italian specialties that might appeal to a broader clientele.

In the 1970s, an explosion of interest in cooking influenced by fresh ingredients and the traditions of different European and Asian cuisines brought still more variety to the pizzeria, as pizzas were served with ever-more-creative combinations of sauces, toppings and cheeses.

This food that has traveled so widely and been embraced by so many cultures continues to evolve. As tastes change and ingredients from kitchens around the world become more widely available, contemporary pizzerias try different pizza and focaccia toppings and calzone fillings, from chicken and spinach enveloped in a creamy

The use of fresh, seasonal vegetables is typical of Italian food. Pictured here is Pizza with Asparagus and Artichokes (page 88).

béchamel sauce to smoked salmon paired with smoked mozzarella and fresh radicchio and shrimp spiced with caramelized garlic.

The recipes included in the following sections of this book represent traditional and modern, typically Italian and innovatively exotic pizza creations, as well as variations on the pizza—focaccia, panini, calzone, mini pizzas and dessert pizzas. No doubt these are not the end of the story in the evolution of the pizza, and other delectable combinations, especially of toppings, are waiting to be found—perhaps by you.

Pizza has an engrossing attraction: from the spectacle of dough whirling through the air, to the luscious smells that emanate from the oven.

CHEESE AND VEGETABLE PIZZAS

Types of Cheeses

For thousands of years, cheese has been one of the most important foods of people throughout the world. The first cheese was probably made more than 4000 years ago by nomadic tribes of Asia. Through the years, knowledge of cheese making spread to Europe, where the world's best-known cheeses originated. Today however, the United States leads the world in cheese production.

There are more than 400 kinds of cheese. They have over 2000 names because some cheeses are known by two or more names. For example, Swiss cheese is also called Emmentaler. Another tendency is for cheeses to take their names from the country or region where they were first produced. Swiss cheese came from Switzerland, and Roquefort cheese is only made near Roquefort, France.

With so many cheeses comes an enormous range of choices in taste, texture and appearance. Some cheeses are soft, but others are hard and crumbly. Some kinds of cheeses taste sweet, and others have a sharp or spicy taste.

An example of a soft cheese included in the recipes of this book is Camembert, originally made in Normandy, France.

Semisoft cheeses include such varieties as blue cheese (such as Roquefort, which is made from sheep's milk; or Gorgonzola, which is made from cow's milk), and, of course, mozzarella. The best loved pizza-making cheese, mozzarella's elastic stringiness only adds to the enjoyment of eating pizza.

Mascarpone is a soft cheese with a creamy texture and is so rich and sweet it is most usually found in desserts.

Hard cheeses include the ever-popular (probably due to its distinctive holes, or "eyes") Swiss cheese and Jarlsberg, its Norwegian relative.

Very hard cheeses include Parmesan. A rich, full-flavored cheese, Parmesan was first made in Parma in northern Italy. Its pungent aroma and crumbly texture make it a perfect addition to Italian meals.

The recipes that follow utilize a wide selection of cheeses, so you are bound to find many that are old favorites, and perhaps others that will provide you with a new experience of cheese.

Some pizzas utilize a combination of cheeses, such as Pizza with Sun-Dried Tomatoes (page 102).

Four Cheese Pizza

Why stop at just one or two? With this one simple meal you can experience four of Italy's favorite cheeses. The sharp flavors of Romano and Parmesan and the smooth textures of provolone and mozzarella prove a great combination.

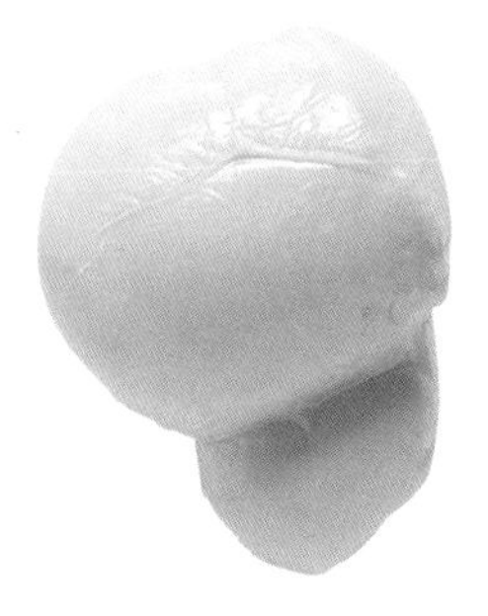

INGREDIENTS

1 quantity Yeast-Free Pizza Dough (page 20)

$1/2$ cup/4 fl oz/125 ml Basic Tomato Sauce (page 34)

2 oz/60 g Romano cheese, grated

2 oz/60 g provolone cheese, sliced

1 oz/30g grated Parmesan cheese

2 oz/60 g grated mozzarella cheese

METHOD FOR MAKING FOUR CHEESE PIZZA

Place a pizza brick, unglazed terracotta tile or baking sheet in the oven. Preheat oven to 450°F/220°C/Gas Mark 6.

On a floured surface, press out the pizza dough using your fingertips into a 9½-in/24-cm circle (always pressing from the inside of the dough to the outside).

Place the pizza dough on the heated brick, tile or baking sheet. Spoon on the tomato sauce and arrange the cheeses on top.

Bake for 15 minutes, or until the pizza is golden on the edges and crisp underneath.

Makes one 9½-in/24-cm pizza
Preparation/Cooking time 30 minutes

The contrasting textures and flavors of the different cheeses add unexpected interest to this cheese-lovers' delight. As with nearly all pizzas, Four Cheese Pizza is best served straight from the oven.

Pizza with Goat Cheese and Zucchini

Imagine a *pastore*, or shepherd, topping a thick piece of bread with his own freshly made goat cheese, a little zucchini and a scattering of leeks. This pizza is a homage to such pastoral combinations.

INGREDIENTS

2 tablespoons extra-virgin olive oil, plus extra for drizzling

1 small zucchini (courgette), trimmed and cut into thin julienne strips

1 leek, white part only, carefully rinsed and thinly sliced crosswise

1 clove garlic, minced

Salt and pepper

1/2 recipe Neapolitan Pizza Dough (page 22), completed through the second rising

All-purpose (plain) flour for dusting

1/4 lb/125 g fresh goat cheese

1 teaspoon dried oregano, crumbled

Juice of 1/2 lemon

METHOD FOR MAKING GOAT CHEESE AND ZUCCHINI PIZZA

Place a pizza brick, unglazed terracotta tile or baking sheet on the lowest rack of an oven. Preheat to 500°F/240°C/Gas Mark 7.

In a large frying pan over medium heat, warm the 2 tablespoons olive oil. Add the zucchini (courgette), leek and garlic and sauté, stirring occasionally, until the vegetables are barely tender, 3–4 minutes. Season to taste with salt and pepper. Remove from the heat. Set aside.

Place the ball of dough on a lightly floured pizza peel or rimless baking sheet. Sprinkle a little more flour on the top of the dough and, using your fingertips, press evenly into a round, flat disk about 1½ in/4 cm thick and 5 in/13 cm in diameter. Lift the dough and gently stretch it with your fingers and then over the backs of your fists, using the weight of the dough to allow it to grow in size. While you are stretching the dough, gently rotate the disk. Continue stretching and rotating the dough until it is about ¼ in/6 mm thick and 9 in/22 cm in diameter and has a rim about ½ in/13 mm thick. Try not to let the center of the disk become too thin in comparison to the edges. Dust the peel or baking sheet with more flour and gently lay the disk in the center.

Distribute the zucchini–leek mixture evenly over the dough. Dot the pizza with the goat cheese and sprinkle with the oregano.

Gently shake the peel or baking sheet back and forth to make sure the pizza has not stuck to it. If it has, gently lift off the stuck section and sprinkle a little more flour underneath. Using the peel or baking sheet like a large spatula, quickly slide the pizza onto the heated brick, tile or baking sheet.

Bake until the edges are golden and crisp, about 8–9 minutes. Remove the pizza with a large metal spatula and slide it onto a dinner plate. Sprinkle with the lemon juice and serve at once.

Makes one 9-in/22-cm pizza
Preparation/Cooking time 30 minutes

Though traditionally made with goat cheese, nowadays feta is often made with cows' milk. It tastes the same and can be used as a substitute for goat cheese.

Italian Cheese Pizza

Deceptively simple, this pizza starts its flavor-hit from the ground up. From the cornmeal of the dough, through the sun-dried tomatoes of the sauce and on to the delicate topping, its layers will tantalize your taste buds.

INGREDIENTS

1 quantity Cornmeal Pizza Dough (page 21)

1/4 cup/2 fl oz/60 ml Sun-Dried Tomato Sauce (page 36)

3 1/2 oz/100 g stracchino cheese or fresh mozzarella, sliced

2 teaspoons fresh or 1 teaspoon dried oregano

METHOD FOR MAKING ITALIAN CHEESE PIZZA

Place a pizza brick, unglazed terracotta tile or baking sheet in the oven. Preheat oven to 450°F/220°C/Gas Mark 6.

On a floured surface, press out the pizza dough using your fingertips into an 8-in/20-cm circle (always pressing from the inside of the dough to the outside).

Place the pizza dough on the heated brick, tile or baking sheet. Spread the tomato sauce over the surface and then top with the cheese and oregano.

Bake for 15 minutes, or until the pizza is golden on the edges and crisp underneath.

Makes one 8-in/20-cm pizza
Preparation/Cooking time 30 minutes

Stracchino (also known as Taleggio) has a mild, delicate flavor. Its cooked, cured version bears a resemblance to mozzarella.

Pizza Margherita

Legend relates that this delicious and patriotic combination was created for Queen Margherita of Italy in 1889 by Don Raffaele Esposito, owner of the era's most famous pizzeria in Naples. Its ingredients honored the colors of her country's flag—red, white and green.

INGREDIENTS

½ recipe Neapolitan Pizza Dough (page 22), completed through the second rising

All-purpose (plain) flour for dusting

⅓ cup/3 fl oz/100 ml Tomato–Basil Sauce (page 38)

6 fresh basil leaves

¼ lb/125 g mozzarella cheese, sliced

METHOD FOR MAKING PIZZA MARGHERITA

Place a pizza brick, unglazed terracotta tile or baking sheet on the lowest rack of an oven. Preheat to 500°F/240°C/Gas Mark 7.

Place the ball of dough on a lightly floured pizza peel or rimless baking sheet. Sprinkle a little more flour on the top of the dough and, using your fingertips, press evenly into a round, flat disk about 1½ in/4 cm thick and 5 in/13 cm in diameter. Lift the dough and gently stretch it with your fingers and then over the backs of your fists, using the weight of the dough to allow it to grow in size. While you are stretching the dough, gently rotate the disk. Continue stretching and rotating the dough until it is about ¼ in/6 mm thick and 9 in/22 cm in diameter and has a rim about ½ in/13 mm thick. Try not to let the center of the disk become too thin in comparison to the edges. Dust the peel or baking sheet with more flour and gently lay the disk in the center.

Place the Tomato–Basil Sauce in the center of the disk. Using the back of a spoon, gently spread the sauce over the dough, leaving a 1-in/2.5-cm border free of sauce. Lay the basil leaves atop the sauce and then arrange the mozzarella slices evenly over all.

Gently shake the peel or baking sheet back and forth to make sure the pizza has not stuck to it. If it has, gently lift off the stuck section and sprinkle a little more flour underneath. Using the peel or baking sheet like a large spatula, quickly slide the pizza onto the heated brick, tile or baking sheet.

Bake until the edges are golden and crisp, around 8–9 minutes. Remove the pizza with a large metal spatula and slide it onto a dinner plate. Serve at once.

Makes one 9-in/22-cm pizza
Preparation/Cooking time around 30 minutes

About Basil

Basileus is the Latin for word for royal, and many cooks regard basil as the royalty among herbs. Basil's culinary dominance is evidenced in its wide use in Italian cooking, bouquet garni, pesto, herbal oils and vinegars and for accenting any tomato dish. It is also used to flavor the liqueur chartreuse.

Native to India, basil has been cultivated in the Mediterranean for thousands of years. Of its approximately 150 species, sweet basil is the most popular; others include bush basil, lemon-scented basil and the holy basil used in Hindu religious ceremonies. Like most herbs, basil has few calories, and reasonable quantities provide a good source of calcium and iron.

The history of basil can be traced to ancient Egypt, where a mixture of basil and myrrh was burned to appease the gods. To the Romans basil signified love. Still today, Italian suitors proclaim their intentions by wearing basil in their hair, and growing basil on windowsills there is thought to attract lovers.

Who knows what might happen if you put it on a pizza?

Goat Cheese, Bell Pepper, Olive and Pesto Pizza

In Italy, traditional home-grown ingredients, such as those used in this recipe, are not blended to disguise the various flavors—instead you can taste the contribution of each to every dish.

INGREDIENTS

1 quantity Yeast-Risen Dough (page 16)

1/4 cup/2 fl oz/60 ml Basic Tomato Sauce (page 34)

1/4 cup/ 2 fl oz/60 ml Pesto (page 42)

6 oz/185 g goat cheese, crumbled

2 red bell peppers (capsicums), grilled, skin removed and cut into strips

3 1/2 oz/100 g black olives, pitted and halved lengthwise

METHOD FOR MAKING GOAT CHEESE, BELL PEPPER, OLIVE AND PESTO PIZZA

Place a pizza brick, unglazed terracotta tile or baking sheet in the oven. Preheat oven to 450°F/220°C/Gas Mark 6.

On a floured surface, press out the pizza dough using your fingertips into a 10-in/25-cm circle (always pressing from the inside of the dough to the outside).

Place the pizza dough on the heated brick, tile or baking sheet. Spread with the tomato sauce, pesto and goat cheese.

Bake for 10 minutes, then remove from the oven and top with strips of red bell pepper (capsicum) in a criss-cross pattern. Place one half of an olive in each square between the pepper. Return to the oven for a further 10 minutes, until the base is cooked through.

Makes one 10-in/25-cm pizza
Preparation/Cooking time 30 minutes

The art of good eating extends to the presentation of food— the more visually appealing a dish, the more enticing it is. Creating a checkerboard pattern adds visual interest to this pizza.

Pizza with Escarole and Pine Nuts

This traditional combination of tender escarole with anchovies, pine nuts and breadcrumbs is found on the tables of rustic pizzerias in Italy and in their more sophisticated counterparts in America and elsewhere.

INGREDIENTS

1/2 cup/4 fl oz/125 ml water

2 tablespoons extra-virgin olive oil, plus extra for drizzling

1/2 head escarole (Batavian endive), tough outer leaves and core removed, coarsely chopped

1 clove garlic, minced

1/2 recipe Neapolitan Pizza Dough (page 22), completed through the second rising

All-purpose (plain) flour for dusting

1/4 lb/125 g Fontina cheese, sliced

2 anchovy fillets, rinsed, patted dry and chopped

1 tablespoon pine nuts

Freshly ground pepper

1 tablespoon toasted fine dried breadcrumbs

METHOD FOR MAKING PIZZA WITH ESCAROLE AND PINE NUTS

In a large frying pan over medium-low heat, combine the water and the 2 tablespoons olive oil. Bring the liquid to a simmer and add the escarole and garlic. Cover and simmer until the escarole is tender, 7 minutes. Transfer it to a colander to drain. When cool enough to handle, squeeze between the palms of your hands to remove as much liquid as possible.

Place a pizza brick, unglazed terracotta tile or baking sheet on the lowest rack of an oven. Preheat to 500°F/240°C/Gas Mark 7.

Place the ball of dough on a lightly floured pizza peel or rimless baking sheet. Sprinkle a little more flour on the top of the dough and, using your fingertips, press evenly into a round, flat disk about 1½ in/4 cm thick and 5 in/13 cm in diameter. Lift the dough and gently stretch it with your fingers and then over the backs of your fists, using the weight of the dough to allow it to grow in size. While you are stretching the dough, gently rotate the disk. Continue stretching and rotating the dough until it is about ¼ in/6 mm thick and 9 in/22 cm in diameter and has a rim about ½ in/13 mm thick. Try not to let the center of the disk become too thin in comparison to the edges. Dust the peel or baking sheet with more flour and gently lay the disk in the center.

Arrange the escarole over the dough. Top evenly with the Fontina, then scatter on the anchovies and pine nuts. Season to taste with pepper. Finish with a drizzle of olive oil.

Gently shake the peel or baking sheet back and forth to make sure the pizza has not stuck to it. If it has, gently lift off the stuck section and sprinkle a little flour underneath. Using the peel or baking sheet like a large spatula, quickly slide the pizza onto the heated brick, tile or baking sheet.

Bake until the edges are golden and crisp, 8–9 minutes. Remove the pizza with a large metal spatula and slide it onto a plate. Scatter the breadcrumbs evenly over the top and serve.

Makes one 9-in/22-cm pizza
Preparation/Cooking time around 30 minutes

Escarole is a variety of endive with loose elongated heads and broad leaves. It has a slightly bitter but pleasant flavor.

Bell Pepper Pizza

In Italian kitchens you can frequently smell peppers being roasted, particularly the sweeter red ones. The soft flesh of lightly roasted peppers gives a melt-in-the-mouth quality to this pizza.

INGREDIENTS

1 large red bell pepper (capsicum)
1 large yellow bell pepper (capsicum)
1 large green bell pepper (capsicum)
1 quantity Wholewheat Pizza Dough (page 21)
2 tablespoons Pesto (page 42)
2 tablespoons grated Parmesan cheese
1 tablespoon pine nuts

METHOD FOR MAKING BELL PEPPER PIZZA

Place a pizza brick, unglazed terracotta tile or baking sheet in the oven. Preheat oven to 450°F/220°C/Gas Mark 6.

Grill the bell peppers (capsicums) until their skin just begins to blister. Place in a plastic bag for 10 minutes and then remove the skin, seeds and membranes. Thinly slice, keeping the different colors separate.

On a floured surface, press out the pizza dough using your fingertips into a 9-in/22-cm circle (always pressing from the inside of the dough to the outside).

Place the pizza dough on the heated brick, tile or baking sheet. Spread the pesto over the surface and then arrange the bell peppers over the top. Sprinkle with the Parmesan and pine nuts.

Bake for 15 minutes, or until the pizza is golden on the edges and crisp underneath.

Makes one 9-in/22-cm pizza
Preparation/Cooking time 50 minutes

Follow this design, or make up your own attractive arrangement of color!

Cornmeal-Crust Pizza

Top this rustic pizza crust with a tangy pesto and goat cheese topping, or any that sounds pleasing. The topping needn't be Italian—the cornmeal suggests Mexican flavors, like spicy chilies.

INGREDIENTS

1 3/4–2 1/4 cups/7–9 oz/220–280 g all-purpose (plain) flour

1 package/2 1/2 teaspoons active dry yeast, with 1/4 teaspoon salt

1 cup warm water (120°F/50°C)

2 tablespoons olive oil or cooking oil

1 cup yellow cornmeal (polenta), and some for sprinkling

Pesto (page 42)

4 ripe plum (Roma) tomatoes, sliced

8 oz/250 g mild goat cheese, crumbled

2 teaspoons chopped fresh rosemary leaves

METHOD FOR MAKING CORNMEAL-CRUST PIZZA

Combine 1 cup/4 oz/125 g of the flour with the yeast and salt. Add warm water and oil. Beat with an electric mixer on low for 30 seconds, then on high for 3 minutes. Stir in the 1 cup/4 oz/ 125 g of cornmeal and the remaining flour.

Turn the dough out onto a lightly floured surface. Knead in enough remaining flour to make a fairly stiff dough that is smooth and elastic, 6–10 minutes. Divide in half. Cover and let rest for 10 minutes.

Grease two 11-in/28-cm pizza pans or large baking sheets. Sprinkle with cornmeal. Roll each half of the dough into an 11-in/28-cm circle. Transfer to prepared pans. Build up edges of dough slightly. Do not let rise.

Prick dough with a fork. Bake in an oven preheated to 425°F/ 210°C/Gas Mark 5 for 7–9 minutes, or until golden brown on edges. Spread each crust with pesto, then top with tomato, goat cheese, rosemary and pepper. Bake for 10–15 minutes more.

Makes two 11-in/28-cm pizzas
Preparation/Cooking time 50 minutes

Some of the best pizza crusts are thin and chewy, like this crunchy cornmeal one.

STEPS FOR MAKING CORNMEAL PIZZA CRUST

STEP 1

Shaping Pizza
Roll out the dough on a lightly floured surface with a rolling pin. Roll from the center out and turn the dough occasionally.

You can refer to Part I for further information on making dough.

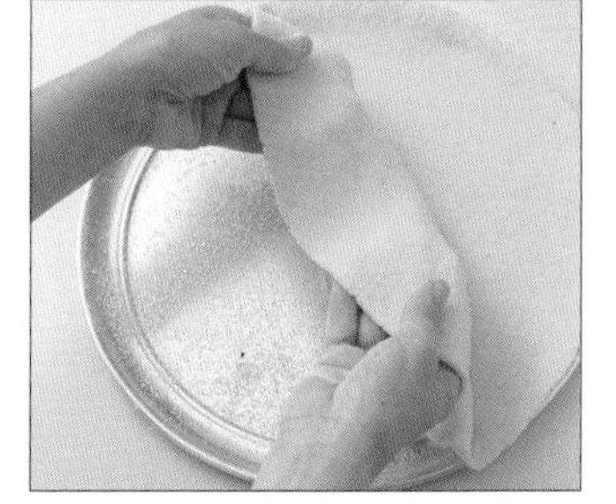

STEP 2

Transferring Dough

Fold the dough in half or quarters and pick it up. Transfer to the prepared pan and unfold to fit, being careful not the stretch it too much.

STEP 3

Pricking Crust

So the dough won't puff up and distort as it bakes, prick it evenly all across with a fork in a regular pattern, as you would a pie crust.

Herb Pizza

Here you get the opportunity to combine all your favorite herbs in one pizza topping. The wonderful taste and aroma of the herbs are complemented by the texture of the poppy seeds.

INGREDIENTS

1 quantity Wholewheat Pizza Dough (page 21)

1 cup/8 fl oz/250 ml Spicy Tomato Sauce (page 36)

1 cup/1 oz/30 g mixed chopped herbs: chervil, rosemary, parsley, oregano, marjoram, chives, basil, as desired

1 tablespoon poppy seeds

3/4 cup/2 1/2 oz/75 g grated mozzarella cheese

METHOD FOR MAKING HERB PIZZA

Place a pizza brick, unglazed terracotta tile or baking sheet in the oven. Preheat oven to 450°F/220°C/Gas Mark 6.

On a floured surface, press out the pizza dough using your fingertips into a 12-in/30-cm circle (always pressing from the inside of the dough to the outside).

Place the pizza dough on the heated brick, tile or baking sheet. Spread the tomato sauce over the surface and then top with the herbs, poppy seeds and mozzarella.

Bake for 15 minutes, or until the pizza is golden on the edges and crisp underneath.

Makes one 12-in/30-cm pizza
Preparation/Cooking time 30 minutes

It is only in comparatively recent times that herbs have been used to flavor dishes. They were first cultivated in monastery gardens because of their healing qualities—and for liqueurs.

Pizza with Yellow Bell Peppers and Capers

This pizza recalls late-night summer meals taken on the large outdoor terraces of country pizzerias in Italy's south. Sweet yellow bell peppers are combined with mozzarella, capers and tomatoes for an exceptionally pretty pizza.

INGREDIENTS

1/2 recipe Neapolitan Pizza Dough (page 22), completed through the second rising

All-purpose (plain) flour for dusting

1/4 lb/125 g mozzarella cheese, sliced

1 ripe plum (Roma) tomato, cut in half lengthwise and then into slices 1/4 in/6 mm thick

1/2 large, meaty yellow bell pepper (capsicum), seeded, deribbed and cut lengthwise into narrow strips

1 teaspoon capers, rinsed and drained

Salt and freshly ground pepper

Extra-virgin olive oil for drizzling

1 tablespoon coarsely chopped fresh flat-leaf (Italian) parsley

METHOD FOR MAKING PIZZA WITH YELLOW BELL PEPPERS AND CAPERS

Place a pizza brick, unglazed terracotta tile or baking sheet on the lowest rack of an oven. Preheat to 500°F/240°C/Gas Mark 7.

Place the ball of dough on a lightly floured pizza peel or rimless baking sheet. Sprinkle a little more flour on the top of the dough and, using your fingertips, press evenly into a round, flat disk about 1½ in/4 cm thick and 5 in/13 cm in diameter. Lift the dough and gently stretch it with your fingers and then over the backs of your fists, using the weight of the dough to allow it to grow in size. While you are stretching the dough, gently rotate the disk. Continue stretching and rotating the dough until it is about ¼ in/6 mm thick and 9 in/22 cm in diameter and has a rim about ½ in/13 mm thick. Try not to let the center of the disk become too thin in comparison to the edges. Dust the peel or baking sheet with more flour and gently lay the disk in the center.

Arrange the mozzarella evenly on the pizza dough. Top with the tomato slices, bell pepper strips and capers. Season to taste with salt and pepper and drizzle with a little olive oil.

Gently shake the peel or baking sheet back and forth to make sure the pizza is not stuck. If it is, gently lift off the stuck section and sprinkle a little flour underneath. Using the peel or baking sheet like a large spatula, quickly slide the pizza onto the hot brick, tile or baking sheet.

Bake until the edges are golden and crisp, 8–9 minutes. Remove the pizza with a large metal spatula and slide it onto a dinner plate. Sprinkle with the parsley, drizzle with additional olive oil and serve at once.

Makes one 9-in/22-cm pizza
Preparation/Cooking time around 25 minutes

Potato Pizza

For something slightly different, let's skip the cheese and tomato sauce. This delicious Potato Pizza is so simple to make, yet such a sensation to eat. A must for all potato lovers.

INGREDIENTS

1 quantity Yeast-Free Pizza Dough (page 20)

1 lb/500 g potatoes

2 tablespoons extra-virgin olive oil

1 tablespoon rosemary leaves

1 teaspoon cracked black pepper

The variety in pizza is not confined to its toppings. For extra fun, cook up a few with different shapes.

METHOD FOR MAKING POTATO PIZZA

Place a pizza brick, unglazed terracotta tile or baking sheet in the oven. Preheat oven to 450°F/220°C/Gas Mark 6.

On a floured surface, press out the pizza dough using your fingertips into a 12-in/30-cm square (always pressing from the inside of the dough to the outside).

Slice the potatoes as thinly as possible.

Place the pizza dough on the heated brick, tile or baking sheet. Brush the base with a little of the oil, then arrange the potatoes on top. Sprinkle with the rosemary and pepper and drizzle over any remaining oil.

Bake for 25 minutes, or until the pizza is golden on the edges and crisp underneath.

Makes one 12-in/30-cm pizza
Preparation/Cooking time 40 minutes

Pizza with Asparagus and Artichokes

It is common to see seasonal offerings in pizzerias throughout Italy. Here, asparagus and artichokes celebrate the arrival of spring.

INGREDIENTS

Ice water

3 baby artichokes, trimmed (see Glossary, page 310) and halved lengthwise

Salt

10 asparagus tips, each about 2 in/5 cm long

3 thin slices yellow onion (optional)

Olive oil, if using onion

4–6 caramelized garlic cloves (see page 116) (optional)

1/2 recipe Neapolitan Pizza Dough (page 22), completed through the second rising

All-purpose (plain) flour for dusting

5 fresh basil leaves, torn into small pieces

3 oz/90 g Fontina cheese, sliced

Freshly ground pepper

2 tablespoons freshly grated Italian Parmesan cheese

1 tablespoon coarsely chopped fresh flat-leaf (Italian) parsley

METHOD FOR MAKING PIZZA WITH ASPARAGUS AND ARTICHOKES

Fill a saucepan three-fourths full with water. Have ready a bowl of ice water. Trim the stems of the artichoke halves even with the bottoms. Add the halves to the saucepan; add salt to taste and bring to a boil. Cook the artichokes until tender when pierced with a knife, about 10 minutes. Remove and immerse in the ice water to halt the cooking. Drain and lay on paper towels to dry.

Ready a second bowl of ice water. Bring a frying pan three-fourths full of lightly salted water to a boil. Add the asparagus tips and blanch for 6–8 seconds. Remove and immerse in the ice water to halt the cooking. Drain and lay on paper towels to dry.

If using the onion slices, in a small frying pan over medium heat, warm enough olive oil to coat the bottom of the pan lightly. Add the onion and sauté until soft, 8–10 minutes. Remove from the heat and set aside. If using the caramelized garlic cloves, prepare as directed on page 116 and set aside.

Place a pizza brick, unglazed terracotta tile or baking sheet on the lowest rack of an oven. Preheat to 500°F/240°C/Gas Mark 7.

Place the dough on a lightly floured pizza peel or rimless baking sheet. Sprinkle on a little more flour and press evenly into a disk about 1½ in/4 cm thick and 5 in/13 cm in diameter. Lift the dough and gently stretch it with your fingers and then over the backs of your fists, using the weight of the dough to allow it to grow in size. Stretch and rotate the dough until it is about ¼ in/6 mm thick and 9 in/22 cm in diameter and has a rim about ½ in/13 mm thick. Try not to let the center of the disk become too thin. Dust the peel or baking sheet with more flour and gently lay the disk in the center.

Arrange the asparagus, artichoke hearts, and onion slices and garlic, if using, evenly atop the dough, then scatter the basil over all. Arrange the Fontina slices evenly over the vegetables, and season to taste with salt and pepper. Gently shake the peel or baking sheet to make sure the pizza has not stuck to it. If it has, gently lift off the stuck section and sprinkle with a little flour underneath. Using the peel or baking sheet like a large spatula, quickly slide the pizza onto the hot pizza brick, tile or baking sheet.

Bake until the edges are golden and crisp, 8–9 minutes. Remove the pizza with a large metal spatula and slide it onto a dinner plate. Sprinkle the Parmesan and parsley evenly over the pizza and serve at once.

Makes one 9-in/22-cm pizza **Preparation/Cooking time** 1 hour

Mushroom Pizza

Mushrooms have been a part of many cuisines for thousands of years. With so many varieties now readily available, this pizza offers you the opportunity to be bold and try some new varieties.

INGREDIENTS

1 quantity Cornmeal Pizza Dough (page 21)

2 tablespoons olive oil

8 oz/250 g assorted mushrooms: cèpes, oyster mushrooms, shiitake mushrooms, straw mushrooms, cultivated mushrooms, sliced if large

1/4 cup/2 fl oz/60 ml Pesto (page 42)

1/2 cup/2 1/2 oz/75 g grated mozzarella cheese

Basil leaves, for serving

METHOD FOR MAKING MUSHROOM PIZZA

Place a pizza brick, unglazed terracotta tile or baking sheet in the oven. Preheat oven to 450°F/220°C/Gas Mark 6.

On a floured surface, press out the pizza dough using your fingertips into an 11-in/28-cm circle (always pressing from the inside of the dough to the outside).

Heat the olive oil over medium heat. Add all of the mushrooms and sauté until almost tender.

Place the pizza dough on the heated brick, tile or baking sheet. Spoon the pesto over the surface and then top with mushrooms. Sprinkle with the mozzarella.

Bake for 15 minutes, or until the pizza is golden on the edges and crisp underneath. Serve sprinkled with the basil leaves.

Makes one 11-in/28 cm pizza
Preparation/Cooking time 35 minutes

The distinctive aroma, flavor and texture of cooked mushrooms make them a delectable addition to many dishes. Here in this Mushroom Pizza, they stand alone in proof of their deliciousness.

Onion Pizza

The cultivation of the humble onion is so ancient and widespread that its precise origins are unkown. The taste of succulent sautéed onions is, however, a familiar favorite for many people.

INGREDIENTS

1 quantity Yeast-Free Pizza Dough (page 20)

2 tablespoons olive oil

1 yellow onion, thinly sliced

1 white onion, thinly sliced

2 red (Spanish) onions, thinly sliced

3 large green (spring) onions, thinly sliced

4 shallots, thinly sliced

3/4 cup/6 fl oz/190 ml Sun-Dried Tomato Sauce (page 36)

METHOD FOR MAKING ONION PIZZA

Place a pizza brick, unglazed terracotta tile or baking sheet in the oven. Preheat oven to 450°F/ 220°C/Gas Mark 6.

On a floured surface, press out the pizza dough to form a 12-in/30-cm circle (always pressing from the inside of the dough to the outside).

Heat the oil in a frying pan, over medium heat. Add all of the sliced onions and the shallots and sauté until just tender.

Place the pizza dough on the heated brick, tile or baking sheet. Spread the Sun-Dried Tomato Sauce over the base and then top with the onions and shallots.

Bake for 15 minutes, or until the pizza is golden on the edges and crisp underneath.

Makes one 12-in/30-cm pizza
Preparation/Cooking time 40 minutes

Pizza with Onion, Anchovies and Olives

Cooks on both the Italian and French Rivieras, from Liguria up through Provence, often combine the sweetness of sautéed onions and full-flavored tomatoes with the sharp bite of anchovy and brine-cured olives.

INGREDIENTS

2 tablespoons extra-virgin olive oil, plus extra for drizzling

1 small yellow onion, thinly sliced

Salt and freshly ground pepper

1/2 recipe Neapolitan Pizza Dough (page 22), completed through the second rising

All-purpose (plain) flour for dusting

4–6 plum (Roma) tomatoes, cut into slices 1/4 in/6 mm thick

5 anchovy fillets, rinsed and patted dry

10 Kalamata or other brine-cured black olives, pitted

1/2 teaspoon dried oregano, crumbled

METHOD FOR MAKING ONION, ANCHOVY AND OLIVE PIZZA

Place a pizza brick, unglazed terracotta tile or baking sheet on the lowest rack of an oven. Preheat to 500°F/240°C/Gas Mark 7.

In a large, heavy frying pan over medium heat, warm the 2 tablespoons olive oil. Add the onion and sauté, stirring occasionally, until completely wilted and golden, about 10 minutes. Season to taste with salt and pepper and then remove from the heat.

Place the ball of dough on a lightly floured pizza peel or rimless baking sheet. Sprinkle a little more flour on the top of the dough and, with your fingertips, press evenly into a round, flat disk about 1½ in/4 cm thick and 5 in/13 cm in diameter. Lift the dough and gently stretch it with your fingers and then over the backs of your fists, using the weight of the dough to allow it to grow in size. While you are stretching the dough, gently rotate the disk. Continue stretching and rotating the dough until it is about ¼ in/6 mm thick and 9 in/22 cm in diameter and has a rim about ½ in/13 mm thick. Try not to let the center of the disk become too thin in comparison to the edges. Dust the peel or baking sheet with more flour and gently lay the disk in the center.

Scatter the onions over the dough. Distribute the sliced tomatoes over the onions. Tear the anchovies into pieces and scatter them over the tomatoes. Finally, top with the olives and oregano. Season to taste with salt and pepper and drizzle with a little extra-virgin olive oil.

Gently shake the peel or baking sheet back and forth to make sure the pizza has not stuck to it. If it has, gently lift off the stuck section and sprinkle a little flour underneath. Using the peel or baking sheet like a large spatula, quickly slide the pizza onto the hot brick, tile or baking sheet.

Bake until the edges are golden and crisp, 8–9 minutes. Remove the pizza with a large metal spatula and slide it onto a dinner plate. Drizzle with additional olive oil and serve at once.

Makes one 9-in/22-cm pizza
Preparation/Cooking time
40 minutes

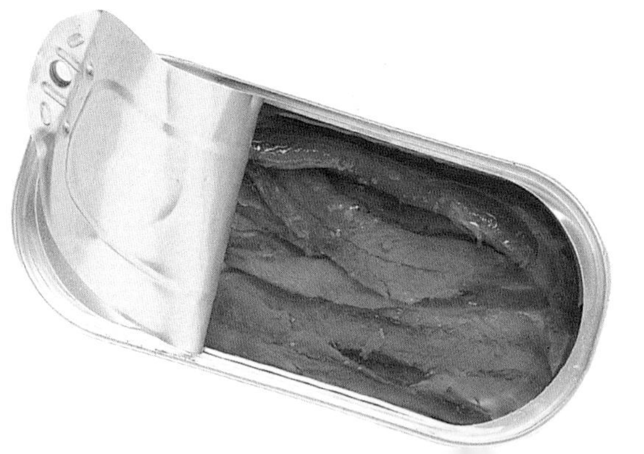

Anchovy is a popularly eaten fish, related to the herring. Anchovies are used to add their highly salty taste to salads, sauces and pizza.

Olive Pizza with Pesto

Experience a vital part of the Mediterranean diet in this pizza. Olives are extensively grown in Italy, Spain and Greece. The olive crop of the United States comes entirely from California.

INGREDIENTS

1 quantity Semolina Pizza Dough (page 19)

1/4 cup/2 fl oz/60 ml Pesto (page 42)

13 oz/410 g pitted, whole mixed olives, such as jumbo black olives, Kalamata olives, Spanish black olives, Spanish green olives

1/2 cup/2 1/2 oz/75 g grated mozzarella cheese

METHOD FOR MAKING OLIVE AND PESTO PIZZA

Place a pizza brick, unglazed terracotta tile or baking sheet in the oven. Preheat oven to 450°F/220°C/Gas Mark 6.

On a floured surface, press out the pizza dough using your fingertips into a 12-in/30-cm circle (always pressing from the inside of the dough to the outside).

Place the pizza dough on the heated brick, tile or baking sheet. Spread with the pesto. Arrange the olives on top and then sprinkle with the mozzarella.

Bake for 15 minutes, or until the pizza is golden on the edges and crisp underneath.

Makes one 12-in/30 cm pizza
Preparation/Cooking time 30 minutes

The saltiness and tang of the variety of olives atop this pizza easily complement its tasty pesto sauce.

Pizza with Sun-Dried Tomatoes

Pumate are the famous sun-dried tomatoes of Apulia, the region tucked into the heel of the Italian boot. Driving along the country roads there, one sees flashes of scarlet on the outsides of many houses. They are plump bunches of Principessa Borghese tomatoes, a variety grown in summer and strung up to dry in the sun throughout the year. Packed in olive oil, they add an intensely sweet tomato flavor to any pizza.

INGREDIENTS

3/4 cup/1 oz/30 g coarsely chopped arugula (rocket)

1 tablespoon extra-virgin olive oil

Salt and coarsely ground pepper

1/2 recipe Neapolitan Pizza Dough (page 22), completed through the second rising

All-purpose (plain) flour for dusting

1 clove garlic

2 fresh plum (Roma) tomatoes, cut into small dice

1/4 cup/2 oz/60 g drained oil-packed sun-dried tomatoes, coarsely chopped and oil reserved

1/4 lb/125 g mozzarella cheese, sliced

2 tablespoons freshly grated Italian Parmesan cheese

METHOD FOR MAKING PIZZA WITH SUN-DRIED TOMATOES

Place a pizza brick, unglazed terracotta tile or baking sheet on the lowest rack of an oven. Preheat to 500°F/240°C/Gas Mark 7.

In a small bowl, stir together the arugula, olive oil, and salt and pepper to taste.

Place the ball of dough on a lightly floured pizza peel or rimless baking sheet. Sprinkle a little more flour on the top of the dough and, using your fingertips, press evenly into a round, flat disk about 1½ in/4 cm thick and 5 in/13 cm in diameter. Lift the dough and gently stretch it with your fingers and then over the backs of your fists, using the weight of the dough to allow it to grow in size. While you are stretching the dough, gently rotate the disk. Continue stretching and rotating the dough until it is about ¼ in/6 mm thick and 9 in/22 cm in diameter and has a rim about ½ in/13 mm thick. Try not to let the center of the disk become too thin in comparison to the edges. Dust the peel or baking sheet with more flour and gently lay the disk in the center.

Pass the garlic clove through a press held over the dough, then rub the garlic evenly over the surface. Top with the fresh and sun-dried tomatoes. Spread the seasoned arugula over the tomatoes and distribute the mozzarella over the top.

Gently shake the peel or baking sheet back and forth to make sure the pizza has not stuck to it. If it has, gently lift off the stuck section and sprinkle a little more flour underneath. Using the peel or baking sheet like a large spatula, quickly slide the pizza onto the hot brick, tile or baking sheet.

Bake until the edges are golden and crisp, 8–9 minutes. Remove the pizza with a large metal spatula and slide it onto a dinner plate. Sprinkle evenly with the Parmesan, drizzle with the oil reserved from the tomatoes and serve at once.

Makes one 9-in/22-cm pizza
Preparation/Cooking time
30 minutes

The piquant and concentrated flavor of sun-dried tomatoes adds a certain richness to all meals that include it. Even the flavorful oil from jars of sun-dried tomatoes enlives dishes, whether a simple salad or when drizzled over Pizza with Sun-Dried Tomatoes.

Swiss Pizza

Add to the international flavor of your pizzas with some typically Swiss combinations of ingredients. Potatoes and cheese are some of the chief products of the country.

INGREDIENTS

1 quantity Wholewheat Pizza Dough (page 21)
1/2 cup/4 fl oz/125 ml Basic Tomato Sauce (page 34)
2 1/2 oz/75g baby new potatoes, thinly sliced
1 small onion, thinly sliced
1 small dill pickle (gherkin), thinly sliced
1 3/4 oz/50 g Swiss or Raclette cheese, thinly sliced

Place a pizza brick, unglazed terracotta tile or baking sheet in the oven. Preheat oven to 450°F/220°C/Gas Mark 6.

On a floured surface, press out the pizza dough using your fingertips into an 11-in/28-cm circle (always pressing from the inside of the dough to the outside).

Place the pizza dough on the heated brick, tile or baking sheet. Spread the tomato sauce over the surface and arrange the potato, onion, pickle (gherkin) and cheese on top.

Bake for 15 minutes, or until the pizza is golden on the edges and crisp underneath.

Makes one 11-in/28-cm pizza
Preparation/Cooking time 30 minutes

The light taste of the Swiss cheese fits well with that of the potatoes, not overwhelming its subtlety. The dill pickles provide a tasty lift to this pizza, along with the Basic Tomato Sauce.

Mexican Bean Pizza

The highly developed agriculture of the Aztecs included corn, beans, tomatoes, avocados and chilies. Mexican Bean Pizza uses these ingredients to bring you a taste of another civilisation.

INGREDIENTS

1 quantity Tortilla Pizza Dough (page 19)

2 tablespoons refried beans

1 large ripe tomato, chopped

2 teaspoons chopped fresh chili

1/2 cup/2 1/2 oz/75 g grated mozzarella cheese

1/2 ripe avocado, mashed, for serving

1 tablespoon sour cream, for serving

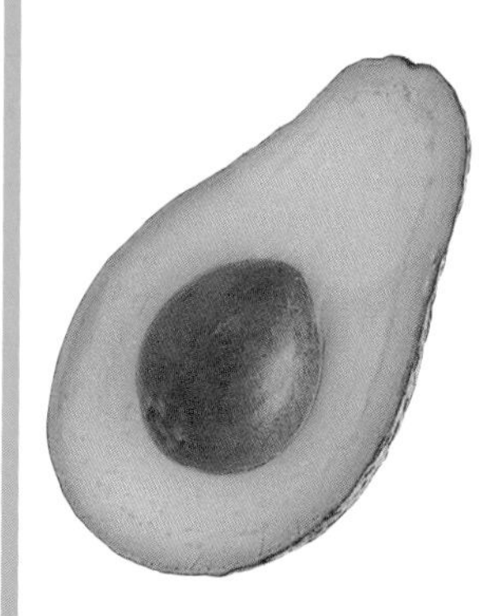

METHOD FOR MAKING MEXICAN BEAN PIZZA

Place a pizza brick, unglazed terracotta tile or baking sheet in the oven. Preheat oven to 450°F/220°C/Gas Mark 6.

On a floured surface, press out the pizza dough using your fingertips into an 8-in/20-cm circle (always pressing from the inside of the dough to the outside).

Place pizza dough on the heated brick, tile or baking sheet. Spread the refried beans over the base. Combine the chopped tomato with the chili and spread over the beans. Top with the mozzarella.

Bake for 15 minutes, or until the pizza is golden on the edges and crisp underneath.

Serve the pizza with the mashed avocado and sour cream.

Makes one 8-in/20-cm pizza
Preparation/Cooking time 30 minutes

Refried beans are beans that have been boiled, fried, mashed and refried. Red kidney beans are one type used in traditional Mexican cooking.

FISH AND SEAFOOD PIZZAS

Mediterranean Seafood

Virtually surrounded by beautiful blue seas—the Mediterranean, the Adriatic, the Ionian, the Tyrrhenian and the Ligurian—Italy's coastline is a paradise of visual and gastronomic delight.

The mild, warm climate, beautiful scenery and historical importance of the Mediterranean region attract millions of tourists yearly. Popular resort areas include the Italian Riviera, as well as the Greek islands and the French Riviera.

The villages and townships that line the Italian coast, and the major cities of Naples, Genoa and Venice that are situated there, all reveal a long and sumptuous tradition of truly splendid seafood cuisine in Italy.

From its vast source, Italy has been able to include a striking range of seafood and fish in many of its dishes.

Perhaps the most famous Italian seafood examples are those *alla Marinara*, with their wonderful combinations of a variety of seafoods that top a pizza or pasta.

Such combinations can include baby octopus, small or large shrimp (prawns), calamari, scallops, oysters, mussels and crabs. Other chief seafoods include anchovies, sardines, salmon, trout and caviar.

With the Mediterranean and other surrounding seas being so heavily fished, the area now carries little large-scale commercial fishing. It does, however, continue to provide an important source of food for the people of the region.

The delicate tastes, textures and colors of seafood give a savory delight to all dishes. And the various shapes and colors add their own visual pleasure.

The recipes that follow reveal some mouth-watering combinations of seafood, with cheeses, herbs and vegetables, on a variety of bases. They cover a wide selection of seafoods to cater for specific favorites.

The early morning bustle of a seafood market reveals it as a popular destination of seafood enthusiasts after the best and freshest fish.

Pizza with Radicchio, Shrimp and Fontina

A study in muted colors and complex flavors, this pizza from Treviso in northern Italy combines two popular regional ingredients, radicchio and Fontina cheese. Tender, pink shrimp are added to enrich the savory dish.

INGREDIENTS

6 cloves garlic

Olive oil, to cover

6 large shrimp (prawns), peeled, deveined and halved lengthwise

1 tablespoon extra-virgin olive oil, plus olive oil for drizzling

Salt and coarsely ground pepper

1/2 recipe Neapolitan Pizza Dough (page 22), completed through the second rising

1/4 head radicchio (red chicory), core removed and coarsely chopped

1 1/2 tablespoons finely shredded fresh basil

4–5 oz/125–155 g Fontina cheese, sliced

METHOD FOR MAKING RADICCHIO, SHRIMP AND FONTINA PIZZA

To make the caramelized garlic, peel the garlic but leave the cloves whole. In a small, heavy saucepan over medium-low heat, combine the garlic cloves with just enough olive oil to cover. Bring to a gentle simmer and cook the garlic until it is covered with golden dots, about 15 minutes. Watch carefully, as the garlic burns easily. Remove from the heat, let cool and then drain off the oil. Set the garlic aside. Reserve the oil for another use such as drizzling over grilled fish or vegetables.

Place a pizza brick, unglazed terracotta tile or baking sheet on the lowest rack of an oven. Preheat to 500°F/240°C/Gas Mark 7.

In a small bowl, mix together the shrimp, 1 tablespoon extra-virgin olive oil, and salt and pepper to taste.

Place the ball of dough on a lightly floured pizza peel or rimless baking sheet. Sprinkle a little more flour on the top of the dough and, using your fingertips, press evenly into a round, flat disk about 1½ in/4 cm thick and 5 in/12 cm in diameter. Lift the dough and gently stretch it with your fingers and then over the backs of your fists, using the weight of the dough to allow it to grow in size. While you are stretching the dough, gently rotate the disk. Continue stretching and rotating the dough until it is about ¼ in/6 mm thick and

Radicchio is a red Italian lettuce with a slightly bitter taste. Its distinctive color and flavor make it a popular addition to a wide variety of salads and meals.

9 in/22 cm in diameter and has a rim about 1/2 in/13 mm thick. Try not to let the center of the disk become too thin in comparison to the edges. Dust the peel or baking sheet with more flour and gently lay the disk in the center.

Scatter the radicchio, garlic and basil evenly over the dough. Top evenly with the cheese and, finally, with the shrimp. Season to taste with salt and pepper and drizzle with a little extra-virgin olive oil.

Shrimp are considered a delicacy in most parts of the world. Fresh shrimp will always have the best flavor and possess a firmer texture than frozen ones.

Gently shake the peel or baking sheet back and forth to make sure the pizza has not stuck to it. If it has, gently lift off the stuck section and sprinkle a little more flour underneath. Using the peel or baking sheet like a large spatula, quickly slide the pizza onto the hot brick, tile or baking sheet.

Bake until the edges are golden and crisp, 8–9 minutes. Remove the pizza with a large metal spatula and slide it onto a dinner plate. Drizzle with extra-virgin olive oil and serve at once.

Makes one 9-in/22-cm pizza
Preparation/Cooking time around 45 minutes

Jumbo Shrimp Pizza

This delicious and simple pizza highlights the shrimps' distinctive flavor. The delicate texture and flavor of the shrimp are here allowed to reveal themselves completely, without the distraction of competing ingredients.

INGREDIENTS

1 quantity Yeast-Risen Pizza Dough (page 16)

1/4 cup/2 fl oz/60 ml Basic Tomato Sauce (page 34)

6 cooked jumbo shrimp (king prawns), shelled and deveined

1/2 cup/2 1/2 oz/75 g grated mozzarella cheese

1/2 teaspoon ground black pepper

1 teaspoon grated lime or lemon zest (rind), plus additional zest for garnish

METHOD FOR MAKING JUMBO SHRIMP PIZZA

Place a pizza brick, unglazed terracotta tile or baking sheet in the oven. Preheat oven to 450°F/220°C/Gas Mark 6.

On a floured surface, press out the pizza dough using your fingertips into an 8-in/20-cm circle (always pressing from the inside of the dough to the outside).

Place the pizza dough on the heated brick, tile or baking sheet. Spread the tomato sauce over the surface and arrange the shrimp (prawns) and mozzarella over the top. Sprinkle with the black pepper and zest (rind).

Bake for 15 minutes, or until the pizza is golden on the edges and crisp underneath. Serve, garnished with the extra zest.

Makes one 8-in/20-cm pizza
Preparation/Cooking time 30 minutes

Here is a shrimp-lover's delight! These plump, large shrimp, preferably fresh from the sea, can evoke—with just one bite —a seaside summer all year round.

Marinara Pizza

At seaside pizzerias all over Italy, treasures from the sea find their way atop the familiar disk of dough. Marinara is one of the best-known and best-loved varieties of pizza.

INGREDIENTS

1 quantity Yeast-Risen Pizza Dough (page 16)

1/2 cup/4 fl oz/125 ml Basic Tomato Sauce (page 34)

8 oz/250g assorted prepared seafood, such as large shrimp (king prawns), mussels, calamari rings, baby octopus, scallops

1/4 cup/1 oz/30g grated mozzarella cheese

METHOD FOR MAKING MARINARA PIZZA

Place a pizza brick, unglazed terracotta tile or baking sheet in the oven. Preheat oven to 450°F/220°C/Gas Mark 6.

On a floured surface, press out the pizza dough using your fingertips into a 9-in/22-cm circle (always pressing from the inside of the dough to the outside).

Place the pizza dough on the heated brick, tile or baking sheet. Spread the tomato sauce over the dough. Arrange the seafood over the top and then sprinkle with the mozzarella.

Bake for 15–20 minutes, or until the pizza is golden on the edges and seafood is cooked.

Makes one 9-in/22-cm pizza
Preparation/Cooking time 30 minutes

All the wonderful flavors, textures, shapes and soft colors of the various types of seafood combine in the ever-popular Marinara to provide the total seafood experience in just one meal.

Pizza with Scallops and Pesto

In this recipe, the intense heat of the oven sears the marinated sea scallops as they sit on a layer of emerald pesto. With Naples and Genoa situated on the coast, the Neapolitan base and Genovese pesto are an appropriate combination.

INGREDIENTS

6 large, plump sea scallops, about 5 oz/155 g total weight, cut in half horizontally if very thick

1 tablespoon extra-virgin olive oil, plus extra for drizzling

Juice of 1/2 lemon

1 tablespoon coarsely chopped fresh flat-leaf (Italian) parsley

2 green (spring) onions, including the pale green tops, thinly sliced

Salt and coarsely ground pepper

1/2 recipe Neapolitan Pizza Dough (page 22), completed through the second rising

All-purpose (plain) flour for dusting

1 clove garlic

1 tablespoon Genovese Pesto (page 40)

METHOD FOR MAKING PIZZA WITH SCALLOPS AND PESTO

In a small bowl, combine the scallops, 1 tablespoon olive oil, lemon juice, parsley, green (spring) onions, and salt and pepper to taste. Stir to mix well, cover and let stand for 20 minutes.

Meanwhile, place a pizza brick, unglazed terracotta tile or baking sheet on the lowest rack of an oven. Preheat to 500°F/260°C/ Gas Mark 7.

Versatile pesto is a delicious seafood accompaniment.

Place the ball of dough on a lightly floured pizza peel or rimless baking sheet. Sprinkle a little more flour on the top of the dough and, using your fingertips, press evenly into a round, flat disk about 1½ in/ 4 cm thick and 5 in/13 cm in diameter. Lift the dough and gently stretch it with your fingers and then over the backs of your fists, using the weight of the dough to allow it to grow in size. While you are stretching the dough, gently rotate the disk. Continue stretching and rotating the dough until it is about ¼ in/6 mm thick and 9 in/22 cm in diameter and has a rim about ½ in/13 mm thick. Try not to let the center of the disk become too thin in comparison to the edges. Dust the peel or baking sheet with more flour and gently lay the disk in the center.

Pass the garlic clove through a press held over the dough, then rub the garlic evenly over the surface. Using the back of a tablespoon, spread the pesto as evenly as possible over the dough. Using a slotted spoon, remove the scallops from their marinade and distribute them over the dough. Sprinkle a little of the marinade over the top.

Gently shake the peel or baking sheet back and forth to make sure the pizza has not stuck. If it has, lift off the stuck section and sprinkle more flour underneath. Using the peel or baking sheet like a large spatula, slide the pizza onto the hot brick, tile or baking sheet.

Bake until the edges are golden and crisp, 8–9 minutes. Remove the pizza with a large metal spatula and slide it onto a plate. Drizzle with olive oil and serve.

Makes one 9-in/22-cm pizza
Preparation/Cooking time around 35 minutes

In this pizza, the soft white and pale pinky-coral of the scallops add lovely color and contrast to the pesto beneath them. The moist, white flesh of this shellfish is best eaten absolutely fresh.

The mild onion flavor of green onions adds the required delicate touch to this pizza.

Crab and Chili Pizza

The delicious, sweet, firm flesh of the crabmeat is here overlaid with strips of creamy brie or smooth mozzarella. Spicy tomato sauce adds a tantalizing tang.

INGREDIENTS

1 quantity Yeast-Risen Pizza Dough (page 16)

1 cup/8 fl oz/250 ml Spicy Tomato Sauce (page 36)

3½ oz/100 g cooked crabmeat

2½ oz/75 g brie or mozzarella cheese, cut into finger-length strips

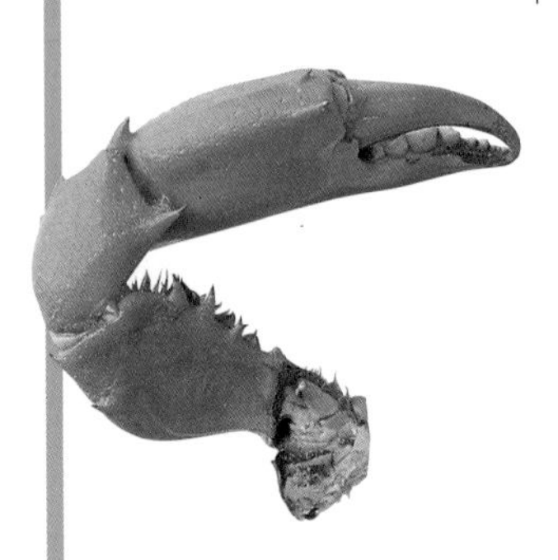

METHOD FOR MAKING CRAB AND CHILI PIZZA

Place a pizza brick, unglazed terracotta tile or baking sheet in the oven. Preheat oven to 450°F/220°C/Gas Mark 6.

On a floured surface, press out the pizza dough using your fingertips into a 7-in/18-cm circle (always pressing from the inside of the dough to the outside).

Place the pizza dough on the heated brick, tile or baking sheet. Spread the tomato sauce over the surface and arrange the crabmeat and cheese on top.

Bake for 15 minutes, or until the pizza is golden on the edges and crisp underneath.

Makes one 7-in/18-cm pizza
Preparation/Cooking time 30 minutes

Achieving a successful blend of ingredients for a pizza doesn't seem so hard when simple combinations produce such great results in aroma, appearance and taste.

Smoked Salmon Pizza

Considered one of the finest flavored fish, salmon is an impressive ingredient for special occasions. With this pizza you and your guests can indulge in the luxury of smoked salmon.

INGREDIENTS

1 quantity Yeast-Free Pizza Dough (page 20)

1/2 cup/4 fl oz/125 g Sun-Dried Tomato Sauce (page 36)

1 oz/30 g pickled onions

3 1/2 oz/100 g smoked salmon slices

1 teaspoon capers

1 teaspoon fresh chervil leaves

METHOD FOR MAKING SMOKED SALMON PIZZA

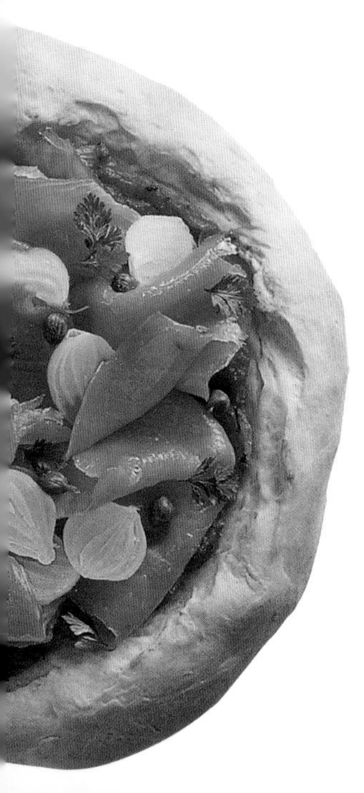

Place a pizza brick, unglazed terracotta tile or baking sheet in the oven. Preheat oven to 450°F/220°C/Gas Mark 6.

On a floured surface, press out the pizza dough using your fingertips into an 11-in/28-cm circle (always pressing from the inside of the dough to the outside).

Place the pizza dough on the heated brick, tile or baking sheet. Spread the tomato sauce over the surface.

Bake for 15 minutes, or until the pizza is golden on the edges and crisp underneath. Allow to cool.

Thinly slice the onions. Arrange them on top of the pizza base with the smoked salmon, capers and chervil. Serve at room temperature.

Makes one 11-in/28-cm pizza
Preparation/Cooking time 1 hour

This pizza utilizes chervil, one of the classic herbs of French cuisine. Its lacy leaves possess a delicate aniseed flavor. Capers are the small pickled buds of a Mediterranean plant and, with the pickled onions, provide a piquant garnish.

Smoked Trout Pizza

Italians love fish and seafood, and trout is a delicacy. Its soft flesh is considered a prize the world over, especially by trout fishing enthusiasts! With this pizza you can sample the distinctive flavor of smoked trout.

INGREDIENTS

1 quantity Yeast-Free Pizza Dough (page 20)

1 small smoked trout

3 large green (spring) onions

1/2 cup/4 fl oz/125 ml Basic Tomato Sauce (page 34)

1/2 cup/2 1/2 oz/75 g grated mozzarella cheese

METHOD FOR MAKING SMOKED TROUT PIZZA

Place a pizza brick, unglazed terracotta tile or baking sheet in the oven. Preheat oven to 450°F/220°C/Gas Mark 6.

On a floured surface, press out the pizza dough using your fingertips into a 10- x 6-in/25- x 15-cm oval (always pressing from the inside of the dough to the outside).

Remove the head, skin and all bones from the trout. Cut the green (spring) onions in half lengthwise and discard the long, green shoots.

Place the pizza dough on the heated brick, tile or baking sheet. Spread the tomato sauce over the base and arrange the trout and onions on top. Top with the mozzarella.

Bake for 15 minutes, or until the pizza is golden on the edges and crisp underneath.

Makes one 10- x 6-in/25- x 15-cm oval pizza
Preparation/Cooking time 35 minutes

Closely related to salmon, trout are native to the cool streams and lakes of the northern hemisphere. Brown trout are native to Europe and west Asia; rainbow trout are native to North America.

Caviar Pizza

To think a humble pizza could bring the ultimate caviar experience! Beluga caviar is the best, with the largest and blackest eggs. However, many varieties of fish eggs, or roe, are available.

INGREDIENTS

1 quantity Sourdough Pizza Dough (page 20)

1 tablespoon Basic Tomato Sauce (page 34)

1 tablespoon crème fraîche

3½ oz/100 g assorted caviars, such as red caviar, black caviar, salmon roe and trout roe

2 hard-cooked eggs, sliced

1 tablespoon chopped chives

METHOD FOR MAKING CAVIAR PIZZA

Place a pizza brick, unglazed terracotta tile or baking sheet in the oven. Preheat oven to 450°F/220°C/Gas Mark 6.

On a floured surface, press out the pizza dough using your fingertips into an 8-in/20-cm circle (always pressing from the inside of the dough to the outside).

Place the pizza dough on the heated brick, tile or baking sheet. Spread the tomato sauce over the surface.

Bake for 15 minutes, or until the pizza is golden on the edges and crisp underneath.

Remove from the oven and top with the crème fraîche, caviar, egg slices and chives. Return to the oven for a few minutes to quickly heat through. Serve immediately.

Makes one 8-in/20-cm pizza
Preparation/Cooking time 35 minutes

The most valuable caviar comes from a type of sturgeon called beluga. Other fine caviar comes from the osetra and sevruga sturgeons. Salmon and trout roe add delicious variety to your Caviar Pizza topping.

Pizza with Smoked Salmon and Mozzarella

This pizza is an inspired American combination of the sophisticated tastes of smoked salmon and smoked mozzarella. A squeeze of fresh lemon and a sprinkling of Italian parsley brighten the assertive flavors.

INGREDIENTS

1/2 recipe Neapolitan Pizza Dough (page 22), completed through the second rising

All-purpose (plain) flour for dusting

2 oz/60 g thinly sliced smoked salmon

1/4 lb/125 g smoked mozzarella cheese, sliced

1 1/2 teaspoons chopped fresh chives

Freshly ground pepper

Extra-virgin olive oil for drizzling

Juice of 1/2 lemon

1 tablespoon coarsely chopped fresh flat-leaf (Italian) parsley

METHOD FOR MAKING SMOKED SALMON AND MOZZARELLA PIZZA

The delicate onion-like flavor of chives complements the salmon.

Place a pizza brick, unglazed terracotta tile or baking sheet on the lowest rack of an oven. Preheat to 500°F/240°C/Gas Mark 7.

Place the ball of dough on a lightly floured pizza peel or rimless baking sheet. Sprinkle a little more flour on the top of the dough and, using your fingertips, press evenly into a round, flat disk about 1½ in/4 cm thick and 5 in/13 cm in diameter. Lift the dough and gently stretch it with your fingers and then over the backs of your fists, using the weight of the dough to allow it to grow in size. While you are stretching the dough, gently rotate the disk. Continue stretching and rotating the dough until it is about ¼ in/6 mm thick and 9 in/22 cm in diameter and has a rim about ½ in/13 mm thick. Try not to let the center of the disk become too thin in comparison to the edges. Dust the peel or baking sheet with more flour and gently lay the disk in the center.

The juice of the lemon adds the necessary tang.

Arrange the smoked salmon on the dough. Top evenly with the smoked mozzarella slices and sprinkle with the chives. Season to taste with pepper. Finish with a drizzle of olive oil.

Gently shake the peel or baking sheet back and forth to make sure the pizza has not stuck to it. If it has, gently lift off the stuck section and sprinkle a little more flour underneath. Using the peel or baking sheet like a large spatula, quickly slide the pizza onto the hot brick, tile or baking sheet.

Bake until the edges are golden and crisp, 8–9 minutes. Remove the pizza with a large metal spatula and slide it onto a dinner plate. Sprinkle the lemon juice and parsley evenly over the top. Drizzle with additional olive oil, if desired, and serve at once.

Makes one 9-in/22-cm pizza
Preparation/Cooking time
30 minutes

Flat-leaf (Italian) parsley possesses a stronger flavor than the curly-leafed variety.

POULTRY AND MEAT PIZZAS

Poultry and Meat

Italian cooking tends to rely more particularly on fresh, good quality vegetables and other staples rather than meat. Pork and veal are the two most popularly consumed meats in Italy but, as a rule, Italians don't eat much meat at all, using it more to add flavor to dishes, rather than as a dish on its own.

The people of the north of Italy tend to eat more meat (and veal is especially favored) than those in the south. In the south, the emphasis of the cuisine is on vegetables, seafood and fish. Lamb is also more common.

Farmers in Italy raise cattle, pigs, chickens and sheep. Every farmer keeps a pig or two to turn into cured hams and salami and other smoked meats, while chicken, rabbit and game add even further variety.

Even with their relatively low consumption of meat, Italians eat more meat than their farmers can produce, so much of their meat is imported from other countries.

As previous sections in this book have shown, pizza works very well without the addition of meat; simple vegetables, seafoods, cheeses and herbs provide an extraordinary variety of choices and delectable combinations.

But, for the meat-lovers of this world, pizza's versatility works brilliantly, revealing once again its ability to complement or enhance one particular ingredient.

The pizza recipes given in this section utilize a variety of meats, including smoked meats such as chicken and turkey, cured meats such as pancetta, prosciutto and salamis—including the popular pepperoni—as well as sausages, pork and bacon. The meats are sometimes combined with cheese and a few other simple ingredients to highlight the taste of the meat, and sometimes with substantial vegetables to round out the flavors.

Salamis and sausages are popular choices for pizza toppings. Particular varieties are immediately familiar, such as chorizo and pepperoni.

Chicken Satay Pizza

Chicken Satay Pizza attests to the pizza's international appeal. Here, satay sauce and bean sprouts lend a delectable Asian flavor. Tender chicken is the perfect topping for the crunchy cornmeal crust.

INGREDIENTS

4 oz/125 g chicken breast fillet

1/3 cup/2 1/2 fl oz/80 ml satay (peanut) sauce

1 tablespoon olive oil

1 quantity Cornmeal Pizza Dough (page 21)

1/4 cup/3/4 oz/25 g bean sprouts

1/2 cup/2 1/2 oz/75 g grated mozzarella cheese

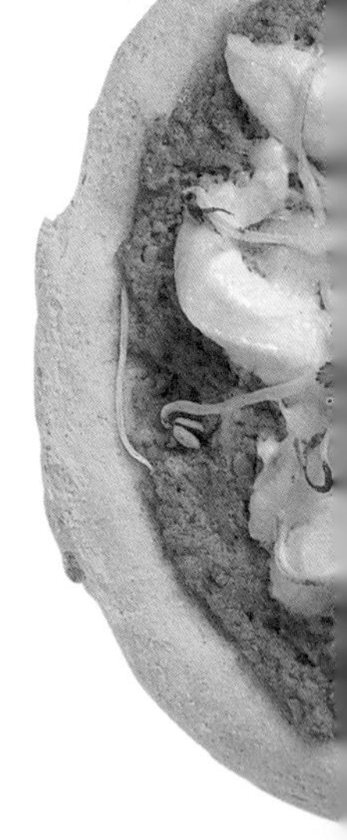

Place a pizza brick, unglazed terracotta tile or baking sheet in the oven. Preheat oven to 450°F/220°C/Gas Mark 6.

Thinly slice the chicken and marinate in 1 tablespoon of the satay sauce and the olive oil for at least 20 minutes.

On a floured surface, press out the pizza dough using your fingertips into a 9-in/22-cm circle (always pressing from the inside of the dough to the outside).

Place the pizza dough on the heated brick, tile or baking sheet. Spread with the remaining satay sauce and then top with the chicken, bean sprouts and mozzarella.

Bake for 15 minutes, or until the pizza is golden on the edges and crisp underneath.

Makes one 9-in/22-cm pizza
Preparation/Cooking time 50 minutes

Though peanuts are native to South America, farmers in Asia and Africa grow about 90 percent of the world's peanut crop. The peanut plant is unusual in that its pods develop underground; hence peanuts are often called groundnuts.

Barbecued Chicken Pan Pizza

Few can resist the attraction of a barbecue, and the distinctive smoky taste of succulent meat that's been cooked in this way. Here is an opportunity to give your pizza that great barbecue taste.

INGREDIENTS

1 quantity Tortilla Pizza Dough (page 19)

1/2 cup/4 fl oz/125 ml Basic Tomato Sauce (page 34)

8 oz/250 g barbecued chicken meat, shredded

1/2 cup/3 1/2 oz/100 g cooked corn kernels

1/4 cup/30 g/1 oz grated mozzarella cheese

1 tablespoon chopped fresh parsley

METHOD FOR MAKING BARBECUED CHICKEN PAN PIZZA

Preheat oven to 450°F/220°C/Gas Mark 6.

On a floured surface, press the pizza dough out to fit a 10-in/25-cm pizza pan (always pressing from the inside of the dough to the outside).

Spread the tomato sauce over the pizza base. Arrange the chicken, corn and mozzarella over the pizza.

Bake for 15 minutes, or until the pizza is golden on the edges and crisp underneath. Serve sprinkled with the parsley.

Makes one 10-in/25-cm pizza
Preparation/Cooking time 30 minutes

Utilizing that old favorite combination of chicken and corn, this pizza is sure to be a success with many family members and guests.

Smoked Turkey Pizza

Italians love celebrating. Turkey calls to mind celebrations—such as Thanksgiving, Christmas and other occasions—that we like to mark with a special meal.

INGREDIENTS

1 quantity Tortilla Pizza Dough (page 19)

1/2 cup/4 fl oz/125 g Basic Tomato Sauce (page 34)

3 1/2 oz/100 g smoked turkey, sliced

1 small onion, thinly sliced

1 tablespoon capers

1 tablespoon redcurrant or cranberry jelly, warmed

The traditional combination of cranberry jelly with turkey works well with the delicious flavor of smoked turkey. The piquant taste of the capers adds a lovely contrast.

Place a pizza brick, unglazed terracotta tile or baking sheet in the oven. Preheat oven to 450°F/ 220°C/Gas Mark 6.

On a floured surface, press out the pizza dough using your fingertips into a 10-in/25-cm circle (always pressing from the inside of the dough to the outside).

Place the pizza dough on the heated brick, tile or baking sheet. Spread the tomato sauce over the base and arrange the smoked turkey, onion and capers over the pizza.

Bake for 15 minutes, or until the pizza is golden on the edges and crisp underneath. Brush with the redcurrant or cranberry jelly and serve.

Makes one 10-in/25-cm pizza
Preparation/Cooking time 30 minutes

Smoked Chicken Pizza

Smoking is one of the oldest methods used to preserve foods. It lends a characteristic flavor to food which has come to be a popularly sought-after quality in itself.

INGREDIENTS

1 quantity Wholewheat Pizza Dough (page 21)

1/2 cup/4 fl oz/125 g Basic Tomato Sauce (page 34)

8 oz/250 g smoked chicken, sliced

3 1/2 oz/100 g goat cheese, crumbled

METHOD FOR MAKING SMOKED CHICKEN PIZZA

Place a pizza brick, unglazed terracotta tile or baking sheet in the oven. Preheat oven to 450°F/220°C/Gas Mark 6.

On a floured surface, press out the pizza dough using your fingertips into an 11-in/28-cm circle (always pressing from the inside of the dough to the outside).

Place the pizza dough on the heated brick, tile or baking sheet. Spoon the tomato sauce over the base and top with the smoked chicken. Arrange the goat cheese on top of the pizza.

Bake for 20 minutes, or until the pizza is golden on the edges and crisp underneath.

Makes one 11-in/28-cm pizza
Preparation/Cooking time 35 minutes

The wholewheat base gives this pizza a rather rustic quality, and combines well with the simple but flavorful topping of goat cheese and smoked chicken.

Chicken and Fennel Pizza

This pizza uses a couple of Italy's favorite vegetables. The aniseed flavor of the fennel adds a distinctive touch to this chicken pizza.

INGREDIENTS

1 quantity Sourdough Pizza Dough (page 20)

2 thin slices fennel bulb

8 asparagus tips

3½ oz/100 g boneless chicken breast

½ cup/4 fl oz/125 ml Basic Tomato Sauce (page 34)

½ cup/2½ oz/75 g grated mozzarella cheese

1 tablespoon olive oil

METHOD FOR MAKING CHICKEN AND FENNEL PIZZA

Place a pizza brick, unglazed terracotta tile or baking sheet in the oven. Preheat oven to 450°F/ 220°C/Gas Mark 6.

Cut each of the fennel slices in half. Blanch the fennel and asparagus in boiling water for 1 minute. Reresh in cold water. Cut the chicken into strips.

On a floured surface, press out the pizza dough using your fingertips into a 11-in/28-cm circle (always pressing from the inside of the dough to the outside).

Place the pizza dough on the heated brick, tile or baking sheet. Spread the tomato sauce over the base and then top with the chicken, asparagus, fennel and mozzarella. Brush the top with the oil.

Bake for 15 minutes, or until the pizza is golden on the edges and crisp underneath.

Makes one 11-in/28-cm pizza
Preparation/Cooking time 30 minutes

Fennel is also known as anise and finocchio, and has been a common ingredient in Italian cooking for centuries. Asparagus was a favorite with the Romans.

Chicken, Oyster Mushroom and Artichoke Pizza

This pizza uses a wonderful combination of typically Italian produce. Its mouth-watering list of ingredients conjures up a quintessentially Italian experience.

INGREDIENTS

1 green bell pepper (capsicum)

1 tablespoon olive oil

1 onion, sliced

1 clove garlic, crushed

5 oz/155 g oyster mushrooms, halved

15 oz/470 g prepared pizza base of your choice

1 1/4 oz/40 ml tomato paste

1 tablespoon extra-virgin olive oil

1 tablespoon chopped fresh basil

1/2 lb/250 g mozzarella cheese, grated

1/2 lb/250 g cooked chicken, sliced

6 oz/185 g jar marinated artichoke hearts, drained

3/4 oz/25 g drained sun-dried tomatoes in oil, sliced

1 oz/30 g drained black olives

Freshly ground black pepper

Extra olive oil (optional)

METHOD FOR MAKING CHICKEN, MUSHROOM AND ARTICHOKE PIZZA

Preheat oven to 500°F/240°C/Gas Mark 7. Quarter the bell pepper (capsicum) and remove seeds and membranes. Broil (grill) the pepper, skin-side up, until skin blisters and blackens. Remove the skin and slice pepper thinly. Heat the oil in a frying pan, add the onion, garlic and mushrooms and cook until onion is soft.

Place the pizza base on a baking sheet and spread with combined tomato paste, olive oil and basil. Top with half the cheese, then the chicken, artichokes, mushroom mixture, bell pepper, tomatoes and olives; top with remaining cheese. Sprinkle with black pepper and drizzle with extra olive oil, if desired.

Bake for about 15 minutes. The topping ingredients for this recipe can be prepared a day ahead; assemble the pizza just before cooking.

Makes one 9-in/22-cm pizza
Preparation/Cooking time 40 minutes

The artichoke, native to the Mediterranean, is a large, edible thistle with a rich, succulent center called the heart.

Four Seasons Pizza

Arguably the most popular pizza in Italy, the *quattro stagioni* pie represents the four seasons in its use of toppings: artichokes for spring, olives for summer, mushrooms for autumn and prosciutto for winter.

INGREDIENTS

PIZZA DOUGH

2 teaspoons active dry yeast

2/3 cup/5 fl oz/160 ml warm water, 105°–115°F/40°–46°C

1/4 teaspoon sugar

2 cups/10 oz/315 g unbleached all-purpose (plain) flour, plus extra for dusting

Salt and ground white pepper

1 tablespoon extra-virgin olive oil

PIZZA SAUCE

1 cup/8 fl oz/250 ml Basic Tomato Sauce (page 34)

2 teaspoons minced garlic

2 teaspoons fresh oregano leaves

1 tablespoon fresh basil leaves

Cornmeal or semolina, for sprinkling

PIZZA TOPPING

2 tablespoons freshly grated good quality Italian Parmesan cheese

3 oz/90 g mozzarella cheese, thinly sliced

3 oz/90 g smoked mozzarella cheese, thinly sliced

4 thin slices prosciutto or baked ham, halved lengthwise

4–8 shiitake, cremini or white mushrooms, stems removed and brushed clean

6 oil-cured black olives, pitted and cut in halves

4 artichoke hearts, quartered lengthwise (drained, canned or thawed, frozen)

olives

Parmesan cheese

artichokes

METHOD FOR MAKING FOUR SEASONS PIZZA

To make the pizza dough, in a small bowl, stir together the yeast, warm water and sugar and let stand until foamy, about 5 minutes.

Place the 2 cups/10 oz/315 g flour, salt and pepper to taste in a mixing bowl or in a food processor fitted with the metal blade. Add the oil, then the yeast mixture while stirring or processing continuously until the mixture begins to gather into a ball.

Transfer the dough to a lightly floured work surface and knead for a few minutes until the dough feels smooth. Form into a ball and place in a bowl. Cover the bowl tightly with plastic wrap and allow the dough to rise in a warm place until doubled, about 1½ hours.

To make the sauce, put 1 cup/ 8 fl oz/250 ml Basic Tomato Sauce in a saucepan and bring to a boil. Add the garlic, oregano and basil, reduce the heat to low and simmer for 2 minutes. Set aside to cool.

Sprinkle some cornmeal or semolina on a rimless baking sheet and, using your fingertips, press and stretch the dough into a round 12 in/30 cm in diameter, forming a slight rim at the dough's edge. Cover with a kitchen towel and let rise again in a warm place until tripled in height, about 1½ hours.

Place a pizza brick, unglazed terracotta tile or baking sheet on the middle rack of an oven. Preheat to 475°F/230°C/Gas Mark 6.

Using a fork, pierce the dough evenly all over to allow steam to escape during cooking.

Spread the tomato sauce over the dough round. Then, for the topping, scatter the Parmesan evenly over the sauce. Place the mozzarella cheeses in an even layer over the Parmesan cheese. Arrange the prosciutto, mushrooms, olives and artichokes on top, overlapping them with the cheeses.

Slide the pizza onto the brick, tile or baking sheet. Immediately reduce the oven temperature to 425°F/210°C/Gas Mark 5 and bake until the dough is cooked and the cheese is light golden brown, 25–30 minutes. Remove the pizza from the oven and let stand for a few minutes before serving.

To serve, slice the pizza into wedges and then transfer to individual plates.

Makes one 12-in/30-cm pizza
Preparation/Cooking time 4 hours (includes pizza dough preparation)

Though representative of seasonal vegetables, this pizza can be enjoyed all year round.

Pancetta Pizza

In the winter months in Italy, farmers are busy preparing their cured and smoked meats and salamis. Pancetta is a delicately flavored Italian bacon.

INGREDIENTS

1 quantity Yeast-Risen Pizza Dough (page 16)

1 cup/8 fl oz/250 ml Basic Tomato Sauce (page 34)

3½ oz/100 g pepperoni, thinly sliced

3½ oz/100 g pancetta or Italian salami, thinly sliced

½ cup/2½ oz/75 g grated mozzarella cheese

METHOD FOR MAKING PANCETTA PIZZA

Place a pizza brick, unglazed terracotta tile or baking sheet in the oven. Preheat oven to 450°F/220°C/Gas Mark 6.

On a floured surface, press out the pizza dough using your fingertips into a 12-in/30-cm circle (always pressing from the inside of the dough to the outside).

Place the pizza dough on the heated brick, tile or baking sheet. Spread the tomato sauce over the surface. Arrange the pepperoni, pancetta and mozzarella over the top.

Bake for 15 minutes, or until the pizza is golden on the edges and crisp underneath.

Makes one 12-in/30-cm pizza
Preparation/Cooking time 30 minutes

Pepperoni is a popular and distinctive Italian salami. Often used as a pizza topping, here it's combined with the more delicate pancetta for a different pepperoni pizza experience.

Tuscan Pizza

Tuscany, in central Italy, is home to the beautiful city of Florence. Tuscany's location allows it to select from the best of both northern and southern Italian cuisine.

INGREDIENTS

1 quantity Cornmeal Pizza Dough (page 21)

3/4 cup/6 fl oz/190 ml Sun-Dried Tomato Sauce (page 36)

6 slices prosciutto

3 1/2 oz/100g smoked mozzarella cheese, thinly sliced

1/4 cup/2 oz/60g sliced roasted red bell pepper (capsicum)

1 tablespoon flat-leaf (Italian) parsley leaves

METHOD FOR MAKING TUSCAN PIZZA

Place a pizza brick, unglazed terracotta tile or baking sheet in the oven. Preheat oven to 450°F/220°C/Gas Mark 6.

On a floured surface, press out the pizza dough using your fingertips into an 11-in/28-cm circle (always pressing from the inside of the dough to the outside).

Place the pizza dough on the heated brick, tile or baking sheet. Spread the tomato sauce over the surface and arrange the prosciutto, mozzarella, bell pepper (capsicum) and parsley over the top.

Bake for 15 minutes or until the pizza is golden on the edges and crisp underneath.

Makes one 11-in/28-cm pizza
Preparation/Cooking time 30 minutes

The cornmeal base adds a pleasingly rustic quality to this meaty pizza. Prosciutto, or Parma ham as it is otherwise called, is a high-quality cured ham originating from an area near the city of Parma in northern Italy.

Japanese-Style Pizza

The traditional flavors of Japan are here presented in a highly unconventional way. The taste, however, attests to pizza's remarkable versatility.

INGREDIENTS

1 quantity Yeast-Free Pizza Dough (page 20)

8 oz/250 g pork fillet

2 tablespoons teriyaki glaze*

Wasabi paste, to taste

1/2 cup/4 fl oz/125 ml Basic Tomato Sauce (page 34)

1/4 cup/1/3 oz/10 g bamboo shoots

1/2 cup/1 3/4 oz/50 g grated mozzarella cheese

1 tablespoon black sesame seeds

*If teriyaki glaze is unavailable, use teriyaki or soy sauce.

METHOD FOR MAKING JAPANESE-STYLE PIZZA

Place a pizza brick, unglazed terracotta tile or baking sheet in the oven. Preheat oven to 450°F/ 230°C/Gas Mark 8.

Trim the pork fillet of any fat and thinly slice. Combine with the teriyaki glaze and set aside to marinate until needed.

On a floured surface, press out the pizza dough using your fingertips into a 12-in/30-cm circle (always pressing from the inside of the dough to the outside).

Place the pizza dough on the heated brick, tile or baking sheet. Spread a little wasabi over the base, then spoon on the tomato sauce. Top with the pork, bamboo shoots, mozzarella and sesame seeds.

Bake for 15 minutes, or until the pizza is golden on the edges and crisp underneath.

Makes one 12-in/30-cm pizza
Preparation/Cooking time 30 minutes

With such exotic ingredients as teriyaki and wasabi, you can't go past this Japanese-style pizza for a truly different pizza experience.

Roast Garlic and Bacon Pizza

This pizza is sure to become a favorite. Tender roasted garlic spreads like soft butter over the pizza, and the strong, salty bacon aroma and taste make this pizza one to remember.

INGREDIENTS

2 whole heads of garlic

4 rashers Canadian (lean) bacon

1 quantity Yeast-Free Pizza Dough (page 20)

3/4 cup/6 fl oz/185 ml Basic Tomato Sauce (page 34)

3/4 cup/3 1/2 oz/110 g grated mozzarella cheese

METHOD FOR MAKING ROAST GARLIC AND BACON PIZZA

Place a pizza brick, unglazed terracotta tile or baking sheet in the oven. Preheat oven to 450°F/ 220°C/Gas Mark 6.

Wrap each head of garlic in foil. Bake for 40–45 minutes, or until tender. Cool slightly, then cut each bulb in half horizontally and press out the pulp.

Trim the bacon of all fat and cut into 3- to 4-in/ 8- to 10-cm pieces.

On a floured surface, press out the pizza dough with your fingertips into a 12-in/30-cm circle (always pressing from the inside of the dough to the outside).

Place the pizza dough on the heated brick, tile or baking sheet. Spread the garlic over the surface and top with tomato sauce. Arrange the bacon over the pizza and then sprinkle with the mozzarella.

Bake for 15 minutes, or until golden and crisp.

Makes one 12-in/30-cm pizza
Preparation/Cooking time 1 hour 30 minutes

If you've never tried roasted garlic, then this pizza provides a great introduction to it. Roasted garlic has a creamy, mild flavor totally unlike that of raw garlic.

Chili, Pepperoni and Anchovy Pizza

This pizza combines three very different and distinctive ingredients. Hot pepperoni, anchovy and mozzarella, traditional Italian fare, are here "all fired up" on the chili–tomato sauce.

INGREDIENTS

1 quantity Yeast-Risen Pizza Dough (page 16)

3/4 cup/6 fl oz/190 ml Spicy Tomato Sauce (page 36)

5 oz/155 g pepperoni, thinly sliced

6 anchovy fillets

1/2 cup/2 1/2 oz/75 g grated mozzarella cheese

METHOD FOR MAKING CHILI, PEPPERONI AND ANCHOVY PIZZA

Place the pizza brick, unglazed terracotta tile or baking sheet in the oven. Preheat oven to 450°F/220°C/Gas Mark 6.

On a floured surface, press out the pizza dough using your fingertips into an 8-in/20-cm circle (always pressing from the inside of the dough to the outside).

Thinly slice the pepperoni.

Place the pizza dough on the heated brick, tile or baking sheet. Spoon the tomato sauce over the base, then arrange the pepperoni, anchovies and mozzarella on the top.

Bake for 20–25 minutes, or until the pizza is golden and the pepperoni is crisp.

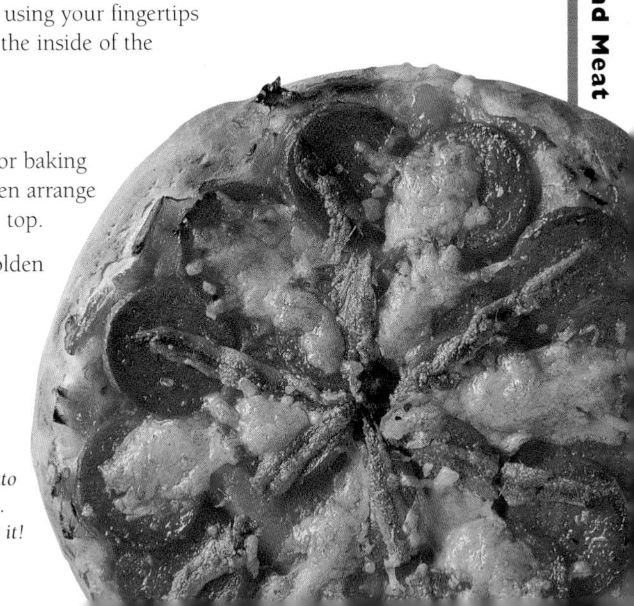

Makes one 8-in/20-cm pizza
Preparation/Cooking time 30 minutes

How many chilies you choose to put in the Spicy Tomato Sauce depends on how hot you think you can handle it. Spare a thought, though, for others who may be eating it!

Pizza with Spinach, Sausage, Salami and Red Bell Pepper

For this pizza, fennel-scented sweet Italian sausages combine well with the other toppings, but choose the type of sausage you prefer.

INGREDIENTS

1 red bell pepper (capsicum)

1 sweet Italian sausage, about 1/4 lb/125 g, casing removed and meat crumbled

1/2 bunch spinach, stems removed

Salt

1/2 recipe Neapolitan Pizza Dough (page 22), completed through the second rising

All-purpose (plain) flour for dusting

1/3 cup/2 1/2 fl oz/80 ml Uncooked Tomato Sauce (page 37)

2 paper-thin slices yellow onion, each cut in half

4 thin slices salami, torn into pieces

1 thin slice prosciutto, coarsely chopped

1/4 lb/125 g mozzarella cheese, sliced

2 tablespoons freshly grated Italian Parmesan cheese

METHOD FOR MAKING SPINACH, SAUSAGE, SALAMI AND RED PEPPER PIZZA

Preheat a broiler (griller) or an oven to 450°F/220°C/ Gas Mark 6. Set the bell pepper (capsicum) on a baking sheet and place in the broiler or oven. Broil (grill) or bake, turning as necessary, until the skin is charred on all sides. Immediately place in a bowl and cover tightly. Let steam until cool, about 15 minutes. Peel off the charred skin, then pull out and discard the stem and seeds. Cut in half lengthwise and trim any white ribs. Cut into long, narrow strips.

Place a pizza brick, unglazed terracotta tile or baking sheet on the lowest rack of an oven. Preheat to 500°F/240°C/ Gas Mark 7.

Place the sausage meat in a small frying pan over medium heat. Sauté, stirring often, until crumbly and cooked through, 10–15 minutes.

Meanwhile, rinse the spinach but do not dry. Place in a saucepan over medium-low heat, sprinkle with salt, cover and cook, turning occasionally, until wilted, 2–4 minutes. Drain and squeeze to remove the liquid. Chop coarsely.

Place the dough on a lightly floured pizza peel or rimless baking sheet. Sprinkle flour on top and press evenly into a round disk about 1½in/4 cm

Make sure you select true English spinach, and not Swiss chard (silverbeet), which is sometimes substituted for it.

thick and 5 in/13 cm in diameter. Lift the dough and stretch with your fingers and then over the backs of your fists, while gently rotating the disk. Continue until the dough is 1/4 in/6 mm thick and 9 in/ 22 cm in diameter and has a rim 1/2 in/ 13 mm thick. Dust the peel or baking sheet with more flour. Lay the disk in the center.

Place the tomato sauce in the center of the disk. Using the back of a spoon, spread the sauce over the dough, leaving a 1-in/2.5-cm border free of sauce. Scatter the cooked sausage over the sauce, then layer on the spinach, bell pepper (capsicum), onion, salami and prosciutto. Top evenly with the mozzarella and dust with the Parmesan.

Gently shake the peel or baking sheet back and forth to make sure the pizza has not stuck. If it has, lift off the stuck section and sprinkle more flour under-neath. Using the peel or baking sheet like a large spatula, quickly slide the pizza onto the hot brick, tile or baking sheet.

Bake until the edges are golden and crisp, 8–9 minutes. Remove and slide onto a dinner plate.

Makes one 9-in/22-cm pizza
Preparation/Cooking time about 1 hour

There are many varieties of salami, and you can choose your favorite to top this pizza.

Pizza with Sausage and Mushrooms

The delicate flavor of the chicken sausage, or the slightly stronger duck, is the perfect accompaniment to the tender mushrooms that top this pizza.

INGREDIENTS

1 chicken or duck sausage, about 1/4 lb/125 g, casing removed and meat crumbled

2 tablespoons extra-virgin olive oil, plus extra for drizzling

1 small yellow onion, thinly sliced

1 cup/3 oz/90 g sliced, stemmed fresh shiitake or portobello mushrooms

1 clove garlic, minced

1 teaspoon minced fresh thyme

Salt and freshly ground pepper

1/2 recipe Neapolitan Pizza Dough (page 22), completed through the second rising

All-purpose (plain) flour for dusting

1/4 lb/125 g mozzarella or Fontina cheese, sliced

2 tablespoons freshly grated Italian Parmesan cheese

METHOD FOR MAKING PIZZA WITH SAUSAGE AND MUSHROOMS

Native to the Mediterranean, thyme improves digestion and its oil, thymol, is antibacterial.

Place the sausage meat in a small frying pan over medium heat and sauté, stirring often, until crumbly and cooked through, 10–15 minutes. Remove from the heat and set aside.

In a large, heavy frying pan over medium heat, warm the 2 tablespoons olive oil. Add the onion and sauté, stirring frequently, until completely wilted, about 10 minutes. Add the mushrooms, garlic and thyme and continue cooking over medium heat until the onions are golden and the mushrooms are tender, about 5 minutes longer. Season to taste with salt and pepper and remove from the heat.

Place a pizza brick, unglazed terracotta tile or baking sheet on the lowest rack of an oven. Preheat to 500°F/240°C/Gas Mark 7.

Place the ball of dough on a lightly floured pizza peel or rimless baking sheet. Sprinkle a little more flour on the top of the dough and, using your fingertips, press evenly into a round, flat disk about 1½ in/4 cm thick and 5 in/13 cm in diameter. Lift the dough and gently stretch it with your fingers and then over the backs of your fists, using the weight of the dough to allow it to grow in size. While you are stretching the dough, gently rotate the disk. Continue stretching and rotating the dough until it is about 1/4 in/6 mm thick and 9 in/22 cm in diameter and has a rim about 1/2 in/13 mm thick. Try not to let the center of the disk become too thin in comparison to the edges.

Dust the peel or baking sheet with more flour and gently lay the disk in the center.

Spread the onion–mushroom mixture evenly over the dough, then scatter on the sausage. Top evenly with the cheese slices.

Gently shake the peel or baking sheet back and forth to make sure the pizza has not stuck to it. If it has, gently lift off the stuck section and sprinkle a little more flour underneath. Using the peel or baking sheet like a large spatula, quickly slide the pizza onto the hot brick, tiles or baking sheet.

Bake until the edges are golden and crisp, 8–9 minutes. Remove the pizza with a large metal spatula and slide it onto a dinner plate. Sprinkle evenly with the Parmesan and serve.

Makes one 9-in/22-cm pizza
Preparation/Cooking time about 45 minutes

Hearty shiitake or portobello mushrooms are delicious when combined with the delicate flavors of this pizza. The final addition of Parmesan cheese adds just the right sharpness.

CALZONE

Calzone

A Neapolitan variation of pizza is the calzone. Originally calzone was a long tube of pizza dough that resembled the *calzone* (pants) that the Neapolitans wore in the nineteenth century.

Today the dough is simply folded over to a half-moon shape and filled with a combination of ingredients such as tomatoes, mozzarella, ricotta and salami.

For family meals it is also common to make many mini calzone, or *calzoncini,* and fry them in oil.

Other times, small plain pieces of pizza dough are dropped into boiling oil and fried. These tiny "*pizzelle*" are brought to the table hot, and are delicious topped with tomato sauce and grated Parmesan cheese.

A small and very popular restaurant in Milan, called Paper Moon, makes a particularly simple version which is highly acclaimed. There is no filling in their calzone, but it is puffed up quite high and covered with a slice of prosciutto which is placed on top at the very last moment, after the calzone is cooked. The recipe was discovered in a very old book belonging to a Neapolitan family.

Calzone with Assorted Meats and Cheeses

This pizza is a variation on some typical calzone recipes. In it, the pungent flavors of salami, prosciutto and mortadella are mellowed by sweet ricotta and Parmesan cheese.

INGREDIENTS

2 tablespoons extra-virgin olive oil

1 small yellow onion, thinly sliced

Salt and freshly ground pepper

1/2 cup/4 oz/125 g ricotta cheese

2 thin slices salami, coarsely chopped

1 slice prosciutto, coarsely chopped

1 slice mortadella, coarsely chopped

1/2 recipe Neapolitan Pizza Dough (page 22), completed through the second rising

All-purpose (plain) flour for dusting

1/4 cup/2 fl oz/60 ml Tomato–Basil Sauce (page 38)

1 tablespoon freshly grated Italian Parmesan cheese

METHOD FOR MAKING CALZONE WITH ASSORTED MEATS AND CHEESES

Place a pizza brick, unglazed terracotta tile or baking sheet on the lowest rack of an oven. Preheat to 500°F/240°C/Gas Mark 7.

In a large, heavy frying pan over medium heat, warm the olive oil. Add the onion and sauté until completely wilted and golden, about 10 minutes. Season to taste with salt and pepper and remove from the heat.

In a bowl, combine the onion, ricotta, salami, prosciutto, mortadella and pepper to taste. Stir to mix well.

Place the ball of dough on a lightly floured pizza peel or rimless baking sheet. Sprinkle a little more flour on the top of the dough and, using your fingertips, press evenly into a round, flat disk about 1½ in/4 cm thick and 5 in/13 cm in diameter. Lift the dough and gently stretch it with your fingers and then over the backs of your fists, using the weight of the dough to allow it to grow in size.

While you are stretching the dough, gently rotate the disk. Continue stretching and rotating the dough until it is about ¼ in/6 mm thick and 8 in/20 cm in diameter. Try not to let the center of the disk become too thin in comparison to the edges. Next, dust the peel or baking sheet with more flour and gently lay the disk in the center.

Ricotta is a creamy cheese which, besides being delicious in cheesecakes, makes an excellent stuffing.

Mound the filling in the center on the half of the dough that is nearest to you. Gently fold the top half of the dough over the filling, stretching and adjusting as necessary so the edges meet. Crimp the edges with a fork to seal. Tear a steam vent about 1 in/2.5 cm long in the center of the top. Spoon the tomato–basil sauce over the vent and spread it around for decoration.

Gently shake the peel or baking sheet back and forth to make sure the calzone has not stuck to it. If it has, lift off the stuck section and sprinkle a little more flour underneath. Using the peel or baking sheet like a large spatula, quickly slide the calzone onto the hot brick, tile or baking sheet. Bake until the top is golden brown and the bottom is dotted with dark brown spots, 8–9 minutes. Remove the calzone with a large metal spatula and place on a plate. Sprinkle the Parmesan over the top and serve.

Makes one calzone
Preparation/Cooking time 40 minutes

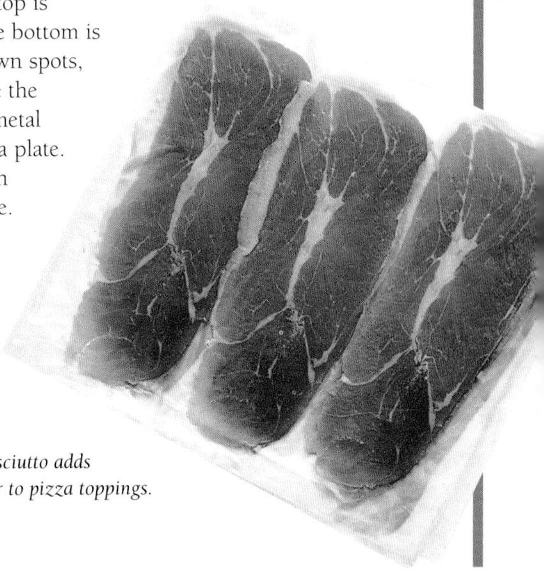

Thinly sliced prosciutto adds texture and flavor to pizza toppings.

Bouillabaisse Calzone

Bouillabaisse is a thick stew, usually made of several kinds of fish and shellfish. This calzone calls for a little adaptation of the traditional bouillabaisse, but the flavor of the dish remains.

INGREDIENTS

21/2 oz/75 g scallops

8 oz/250 g mussels in the shell

3 1/2 oz/100 g shelled jumbo shrimp (king prawns)

1/2 cup/4 fl oz/125 ml Basic Tomato Sauce (page 34)

1/2 teaspoon saffron threads

2 quantities Semolina Pizza Dough (page 19)

METHOD FOR MAKING BOUILLABAISSE CALZONE

Place a pizza brick, unglazed terracotta tile or baking sheet in the oven. Preheat oven to 450°F/230°C/Gas Mark 6. Clean the scallops and mussels. Remove beards, drop into boiling water and cook for 2 minutes. Discard any unopened shells. Remove meat from shells and place in a saucepan with the shrimp, tomato sauce and saffron. Cook over a gentle heat until the seafood is cooked, about 5 minutes.

On a floured surface, press each pizza dough out to form a 9-in/22-cm circle (always pressing from the inside of the dough to the outside). Divide the filling, placing it on one side of each circle. Fold over each round of dough to form a semicircle and press to seal the edges. Cut two holes in the top of each. Place the calzones on the heated brick, tile or baking sheet. Bake for 20 minutes, or until golden on top and crisp underneath.

Makes two calzones
Preparation/Cooking time 40 minutes

Saffron, a common ingredient of bouillabaisse, is the most expensive spice in the world. It is still hand-harvested, just as it was thousands of years ago.

Calzone with Eggplant, Pancetta and Mozzarella

Easily grown by nearly anyone with a bit of sun and a patch of earth, eggplant and tomatoes have long been staples of southern Italian cooking. Pancetta and mozzarella add a rich touch to this savory calzone.

INGREDIENTS

1/4 cup/2 fl oz/60 ml extra-virgin olive oil

2 tablespoons coarsely chopped pancetta or thick-cut bacon

2 Asian (slender) eggplants (aubergines), ends trimmed, peeled and diced

Salt and coarsely ground pepper

All-purpose (plain) flour for dusting

1/2 recipe Neapolitan Pizza Dough (page 22), completed through the second rising

1 1/2 teaspoons finely shredded fresh basil

3 oz/90 g mozzarella cheese, sliced

1/3 cup/2 1/2 fl oz/80 ml Tomato–Basil Sauce (page 38)

METHOD FOR MAKING CALZONE WITH EGGPLANT, PANCETTA AND MOZZARE

Pancetta is an unsmoked Italian bacon that is simply cured with salt and pepper.

Place a pizza brick, unglazed terracotta tile or baking sheet on the lowest rack of an oven. Preheat to 500°F/240°C/Gas Mark 7

In a large frying pan over medium-low heat, warm the olive oil. Add the pancetta or bacon and sauté, stirring occasionally, until it has rendered its fat, about 5 minutes. Add the eggplants and increase the heat to medium. Sauté until the eggplants are golden brown and tender, 4–5 minutes. Season to taste with salt and pepper and remove from the heat.

Place the ball of dough on a lightly floured pizza peel or rimless baking sheet. Sprinkle a little more flour on the top of the dough and, using your fingertips, press evenly into a round, flat disk about 1½ in/4 cm thick and 5 in/13 cm in diameter. Lift the dough and gently stretch it with your fingers and then over the backs of your fists, using the weight of the dough to allow it to grow in size. While you are stretching the dough, gently rotate the disk. Continue stretching and rotating the dough until it is about ¼ in/6 mm thick

The skin of the egg-plant (aubergine) can be purple or white.

and 8 in/20 cm in diameter. Try not to let the center of the disk become too thin in comparison to the edges. Dust the peel or baking sheet with some more flour and gently lay the disk in the center.

Mound the eggplant mixture in the center on the half of the dough that is nearest to you. Top with the basil, mozzarella and tomato–basil sauce. Gently fold the top half of the dough over the filling, stretching and adjusting as necessary so the edges meet. Crimp the edges with a fork to seal. Tear a steam vent about 1 in/2.5 cm long in the center of the top.

Gently shake the peel or baking sheet back and forth to make sure the calzone has not stuck to it. If it has, gently lift off the stuck section and sprinkle a little more flour underneath. Using the peel or baking sheet like a large spatula, quickly slide the calzone onto the hot pizza stone or tiles.

Bake until the top is golden brown and the bottom is dotted with dark brown spots. Remove the calzone with a large metal spatula and place on a plate.

Makes one calzone
Preparation/Cooking time
40 minutes

Mozzarella is easily recognized by its characteristic pear shape.

Calzone with Chicken and Spinach

While not a traditional ingredient in Italian pizzerias, chicken has been embraced by pizza cooks outside of Italy. Here, a creamy filling of tender meat, spinach and prosciutto is tucked into a calzone for an especially rich treat.

INGREDIENTS

1 chicken thigh

Salt and freshly ground pepper

BÉCHAMEL SAUCE

1/2 cup/4 fl oz/125 ml milk

1 tablespoon unsalted butter

1 tablespoon all-purpose (plain) flour

Salt and freshly ground pepper

FILLING

1 bunch spinach, stems removed

1 thin slice prosciutto, chopped

2 tablespoons freshly grated Italian Parmesan cheese

1/2 recipe Neapolitan Pizza Dough (page 22), completed through the second rising

All-purpose (plain) flour for dusting

METHOD FOR MAKING CALZONE WITH CHICKEN AND SPINACH

Preheat an oven to 400°F/200°C/Gas Mark 7. Place the chicken thigh in a baking pan and season with salt and pepper. Roast until golden brown and the juices run clear when the meat is pricked with a knife, 25–30 minutes. Remove and discard the skin and bone and shred the meat.

To make the béchamel sauce, heat the milk in a small saucepan over medium-low heat until small bubbles appear along the pan edge. In another small saucepan over medium-low heat, melt the butter. Add the flour and whisk to form a smooth paste. Reduce the heat to low and cook, stirring, for about 2 minutes. When the milk is hot, add the butter–flour mixture, whisking constantly until it begins to simmer. Simmer over medium heat until the sauce thickens enough to coat a spoon, about 20 minutes. Season with salt and pepper. Set aside until needed.

Rinse the spinach but do not dry. Place in a saucepan over medium-low heat, cover and cook, turning occasionally, until wilted, 2–4 minutes. Drain and squeeze to remove the liquid. Chop coarsely.

Place a pizza brick, unglazed terracotta tile or baking sheet on the lowest rack of an oven. Preheat to 500°F/240°C/Gas Mark 7.

In a bowl, combine the shredded chicken, spinach, béchamel, prosciutto and Parmesan. Stir to mix well.

Place the dough on a floured pizza peel or rimless baking sheet. Sprinkle more flour on top and press evenly into a round disk 1½ in/4 cm thick and 5 in/13 cm in diameter. Lift the dough and stretch with your fingers and then over the backs of your fists while gently rotating the disk. Continue until the dough is ¼ in/6 mm thick and 8 in/20 cm in diameter. Dust the peel or baking sheet with flour and lay the disk in the center.

Mound the filling in the center of the half of the dough that is nearest to you and fold over the filling, stretching as necessary so the edges meet. Crimp the edges to seal. Tear a vent 1 in/2.5 cm long in the center of the top.

Using the peel or baking sheet like a large spatula, quickly slide the calzone onto the hot brick, tile or baking sheet. Bake until the top is golden brown, 8–9 minutes. Serve immediately.

Makes one calzone
Preparation/Cooking time 50 minutes

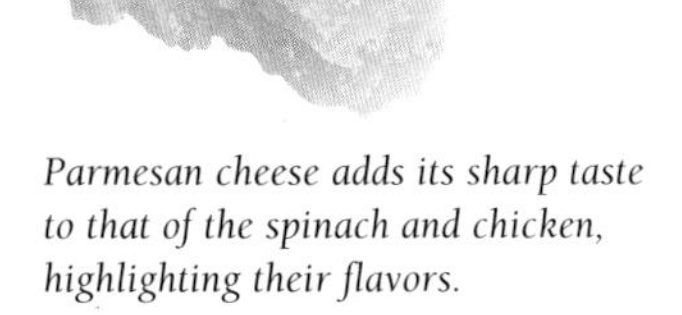

Parmesan cheese adds its sharp taste to that of the spinach and chicken, highlighting their flavors.

FOCACCIA AND PANINI

Focaccia and Panini

Although the name varies from region to region, focaccia (which means "cake" or "bun") is found throughout Italy. In Liguria the *focaccerie* bake it drizzled with olive oil and sprinkled with salt or topped with sweet onions or black olives. In Tuscany they call it *schiacciata* (meaning "crushed" or "flattened") and flavor it with herbs. *Fugazza* is the Venetian word for focaccia, and this recipe includes sugar, eggs and a splash of sweet spirit such as rum.

Focaccia is a natural choice for constructing *panini*, the little sandwiches of Italy. The rustic charm and appealing texture of the bread inspire many filling combinations, from a vegetarian ensemble of eggplant, tomatoes, mozzarella and basil to a more distinctive filling of halibut, arugula and delicious roasted peppers.

Focaccia and panini are made from a softer, more yeasty dough than pizza and, unlike pizza, are usually served warm or at room temperature. Seasoned with herbs and sprinkled with coarse salt, sharp cheese or assorted other piquant condiments, they make a very satisfying light meal.

For an extra flavorful olive oil, use extra-virgin for dipping.

Focaccia

This rustic Italian flat bread is here topped with a simple but ultimately rich combination of pine nuts, black olives and Parmesan cheese. Warm some additional olive oil to dip the slices in if you like; the tiny dimples on the surface of the focaccia trap the flavorful oil.

INGREDIENTS

CALZONE DOUGH

2 3/4–3 1/4 cups/11–12 1/2 oz/340–400 g all-purpose (plain) flour

2 1/2 teaspoons active dry yeast

1/4 teaspoon salt

2 tablespoons snipped fresh rosemary or thyme, or 2 teaspoons dried rosemary or thyme, crushed

1 cup warm water (120–130°F/50–55°C)

2 tablespoons olive oil

PIZZA TOPPING

2 cloves garlic, minced

2 tablespoons olive oil

1 cup chopped, pitted ripe olives, halved lengthwise

1/4 cup pine nuts or chopped walnuts

1/4 cup shredded Parmesan cheese

1/2 teaspoon black pepper (optional)

Olive oil (optional)

METHOD FOR MAKING FOCACCIA

For calzone dough, in a large bowl stir together 1¼ cups of flour, the yeast and salt. Add the herbs, garlic, water and oil. Beat with an electric mixer on low speed for 30 seconds, scraping the bowl constantly. Beat on high speed for 3 minutes. Using a wooden spoon, stir in as much of the remaining flour as you can. Turn the dough out onto a lightly floured surface. Knead in enough of the remaining flour to make a moderately stiff dough that is smooth and elastic (6–8 minutes total). Divide in half. Cover and let rest for 10 minutes.

Preheat an oven to 450°F/ 220°C/Gas Mark 6.

Firm black olives add an inviting aroma as well as a decorative look to this focaccia.

Grease a 15 x 10 x 1 in/ 38 x 25 x 2.5 cm baking pan. Roll or pat the dough into the pan. Press slight indentations into the dough with your fingertips. Brush the dough with 2 tablespoons oil. Press the olives into the indentations. Sprinkle with nuts and Parmesan cheese. If desired, sprinkle with black pepper. Cover and let rise in a warm place for 15 minutes.

Bake in a preheated oven for 12 to 15 minutes, or till golden brown. Serve warm, cut into squares or rectangles. If desired, serve with additional olive oil.

Makes one 15 x 10-in/38 x 25cm focaccia
Preparation/Cooking time 1 hour

STEPS FOR MAKING FOCACCIA

Remember to pull or roll from the center outwards to achieve an even thickness.

STEP 1

Shaping Dough

Whether you choose to shape your focaccia into a circle, rectangle or square, simply place the dough in a lightly oiled baking pan. Use a rolling pin to stretch it until it fully covers the bottom of the pan. Or, pat it into the desired shape.

The indentations you make with your fingers need only be 1/2 in/ 13mm deep.

STEP 2

Making Indents

Once the dough is in the pan, use your fingertips to dot the dough with slight indentations. Press straight down, not at a slant, for best effect.

Focaccia with Coarse Salt

In pizzerias, this simple focaccia is sometimes served with a tumbler of light red wine before dinner. It can also be split in half and used to house a variety of fillings for your own panini creations.

INGREDIENTS

1/2 recipe Herb-Flavored Focaccia dough (page 26), completed through the first rising

1 1/2 teaspoons coarse salt

Coarsely ground pepper

1 1/2 tablespoons coarsely chopped fresh rosemary

Extra-virgin olive oil for drizzling

METHOD FOR MAKING FOCACCIA WITH COARSE SALT

Lightly oil an 8-in/20-cm round cake pan or similar pan. Place the dough in the prepared pan and gently stretch it to the edges, pulling it from the center outward to achieve an even thickness. If the dough springs back toward the center and is difficult to work with, cover and set it aside to relax for 10 minutes, then continue coaxing the dough out to an even thickness. Cover with a kitchen towel and let rise until almost doubled in bulk and very soft and puffy, about 45 minutes.

Preheat an oven to 475°F/230°C/Gas Mark 6.

Italian extra-virgin olive oil has its own distinctive, fruity flavor.

Using your fingertips, dimple the dough vigorously in several places, leaving indentations about 1/2 in/13 mm deep. Again cover the pan with a towel and let rise for 20 minutes longer.

Sprinkle the risen dough evenly with the salt and pepper to taste and the rosemary. Drizzle with olive oil. Bake until golden brown and cooked through, 15–18 minutes. Transfer the pan to a rack and let stand until the focaccia is barely warm, about 10 minutes, then serve.

Makes one 8-in/20-cm round
Preparation/Cooking time just over 2 hours

About Rosemary

Rosemary is one of the highlights of the herb or kitchen garden. Native to the Mediterranean, it has a popular place in Italian, French and Greek cuisines. Its sweet, strong flavor goes particularly well with lamb, as well as with vegetables.

Rosemary's name comes from the Latin word *rosmarinus*, meaning "sea dew", and it loves to grow by the sea. Later it was called Rose of Mary, or rosemary, in honor of the Virgin Mary.

The scent of rosemary stays on the fingers a long time after it has been touched; this may be the reason that it is widely known as the symbol of remembrance. Europeans carried rosemary (and sometimes still do) at weddings and funerals because they believed it would aid their memories of promises and people.

Rosemary oil is used in perfumes. Rosemary is also known for its pest-repellent and medicinal properties: the dried leaves have been used in sachets to repel moths, and to brew tea for stomach aches and headaches.

Eggplant Focaccia

This focaccia presents you with the delicious combination of eggplant (aubergine), sun-dried tomato and basil—all typical Italian ingredients. Once again, a simple combination proves a great success!

INGREDIENTS

1 medium/6 1/2 oz/200g eggplant (aubergine)

1 tablespoon olive oil

1 round Herb-Flavored Focaccia (page 26)

1/2 cup/4 fl oz/125 ml Sun-Dried Tomato Sauce (page 36)

1 teaspoon fresh basil leaves, roughly torn

1 3/4 oz/50 g Provolone cheese, grated

Place a pizza brick, unglazed terracotta tile or baking sheet in the oven. Preheat oven to 450°F/220°C/Gas Mark 6.

Thinly slice the eggplant (aubergine). Brush both sides of the eggplant with some of the olive oil and broil (grill) until browned on both sides.

Place the precooked focaccia (*see recipe on page 26*) on the heated brick, tile or baking sheet. Spread the focaccia with the tomato sauce and then top with the eggplant, basil and Provolone.

Bake for 10 minutes, or until heated through.

Makes one 8-in/20-cm focaccia
Preparation/Cooking time 25 minutes

Focaccia with Onions, Walnuts and Gorgonzola

Cut into thin slices or squares, this focaccia makes a marvelous addition to a simple antipasto accompanied with a glass of *vino da tavola*. Gorgonzola dolcelatte is a blue cheese that is sweeter and milder than Gorgonzola piccante.

INGREDIENTS

1/2 recipe Herb-Flavored Focaccia dough (page 26), completed through the first rising

2 tablespoons extra-virgin olive oil

1/2 large yellow onion, thinly sliced

3 oz/90 g Gorgonzola dolcelatte cheese, coarsely chopped

1/4 cup/1 oz/30 g coarsely chopped walnuts

METHOD FOR MAKING FOCACCIA WITH ONION, WALNUT AND GORGONZOLA

Lightly oil an 8-in/20-cm round cake pan or similar pan. Place the dough in the prepared pan and gently stretch it to the edges, pulling it from the center outward to achieve an even thickness. If the dough springs back toward the center and is difficult to work with, cover and set it aside to relax for 10 minutes, then continue coaxing the dough out to an even thickness. Cover with a kitchen towel and let rise until almost doubled in bulk and very soft and puffy, about 45 minutes.

While the dough is rising, in a frying pan over medium-low heat, warm the olive oil. Add the onion and sauté until golden brown and very soft and sweet, about 20 minutes. Remove from the heat and let cool.

Preheat an oven to 475°F/230°C/Gas Mark 6.

Using your fingertips, dimple the dough vigorously in several places, leaving indentations about 1/2 in/13 mm deep. Again cover the pan with a towel and let rise for 20 minutes longer.

Spread the cooked onion evenly over the risen dough. Scatter the Gorgonzola over the onion. Top with the walnuts. Bake until golden brown and cooked through, 15–18 minutes. Transfer the pan to a rack and let stand until the focaccia is barely warm, about 10 minutes, then serve.

Makes one 8-in/20-cm focaccia
Preparation/Cooking time just over 2 hours

About Walnuts

Walnuts' distinctive flavor has made them a popular addition to both the sweet and savory dishes of many countries. They add a wonderful variety to salads and other meals (as well as to chocolate and confectionery), and they are equally delicious when eaten on their own, either raw or roasted. Their taste and texture make a pleasing complement to many pizza toppings, too.

English, or Persian, walnut trees have been grown commercially in Europe since ancient times. They are large, spreading trees that grow up to about 100 feet (30 m) tall, and possess gray bark, large leaves and soft wood (which is often used to make furniture). These days, the United States leads the world in the production of walnuts. Other major walnut-growing countries include China, Greece and Turkey.

Walnuts are a good source of protein (which makes them very beneficial to vegetarian diets), fiber, and B and E vitamins, and most of their fat content is polyunsaturated. Walnuts are therefore another healthy addition to any meal.

Artichoke and Tomato Focaccia

Tender artichoke hearts and ripe tomatoes (once known as love apples) are here combined with tasty pesto, the basis of which is basil — known in legend as the herb that signifies love.

INGREDIENTS

1/2 cup/4 fl oz/125 ml Basic Tomato Sauce (page 34)

1 tablespoon Pesto (page 42)

1 round Herb-Flavored Focaccia (page 26)

2 plum (Roma) tomatoes, sliced

2 small balls fresh mozzarella cheese (bocconcini), sliced

2 marinated artichoke hearts, quartered

1 3/4 oz/50 g Parmesan cheese, thinly sliced

METHOD FOR MAKING ARTICHOKE AND TOMATO FOCACCIA

Place a pizza brick, unglazed terracotta tile or baking sheet in the oven. Preheat oven to 450°F/220°C/Gas Mark 6.

Combine the tomato sauce and pesto.

Place the focaccia on the heated brick, tile or baking sheet. Spread the mixed sauces over the focaccia. Top with the tomatoes, mozzarella slices and artichokes. Arrange the Parmesan over the top.

Bake for 15 minutes, or until heated through.

Makes one 8-in/20-cm focaccia
Preparation/Cooking time 25 minutes

Focaccia with Cheese

Taleggio is a soft, creamy Italian cheese with a hint of acidic tang. It melts beautifully atop this savory focaccia. For the Taleggio, you may substitute a good-quality Jack cheese or Fontina.

INGREDIENTS

½ recipe Herb-Flavored Focaccia dough (page 26), completed through the first rising

2 oz/60 g Taleggio cheese, coarsely chopped

10 fresh sage leaves

Salt and freshly ground pepper

Extra-virgin olive oil for drizzling

METHOD FOR MAKING FOCACCIA WITH CHEESE

Lightly oil an 8-in/20-cm round cake pan or similar pan. Place the dough in the prepared pan and gently stretch it to the edges, pulling it from the center outward to achieve an even thickness. If the dough springs back toward the center and is difficult to work with, cover and set it aside to relax for 10 minutes, then continue coaxing the dough out to an even thickness. Cover with a kitchen towel and let rise until almost doubled in bulk and very soft and puffy, about 45 minutes.

Preheat an oven to 475°F/230°C/Gas Mark 6.

Using your fingertips, dimple the dough vigorously in several places, leaving indentations about 1/2 in/13 mm deep. Again cover the pan with a towel and let the dough rise for another 20 minutes.

Top the risen dough evenly with the Taleggio cheese, sage and salt and pepper to taste. Drizzle the top with olive oil, making sure to coat the sage leaves evenly. Bake until golden brown and cooked through, 15–18 minutes. Transfer the pan to a rack and let stand until the focaccia is barely warm, about 10 minutes, then serve.

Makes one 8-in/20-cm focaccia
Preparation/Cooking time just over 2 hours

About Sage

Sage's bitter-tasting leaves provide an important herb for cooking. Sage is known for its strong odor; some say its smell resembles that of camphor. Traditionally, cooks use the gray-green leaves and stems of common sage in making stuffings, seasonings for sausages and cheeses, dressings for meat and in sauces. Sage also delivers its warm pungency to vegetables and, in the recipe on page 215, to a delicious pizza.

Sage, like many herbs, has medicinal properties. The name itself originates from the Latin *salvare*, meaning "to save". It was used in Crete as early as 1600 BC to clear throat inflammation. It is now used to fight colds and flu. It also reduces sweating, decreases saliva production and its tea is said to lower blood sugar. Sage has strong antioxidant and antibacterial qualities, and is used in cooking not only for flavor but also to help preserve foods.

An important herb native to the Mediterranean, it is also popular in the Middle East and the United States.

Focaccia with Red Onion

This focaccia is found on the menus of pizzerias in Florence, where small, three-wheel flatbed trucks laden with torpedo-shaped purple onions—their tops flopping over the edge of the bed—zoom into the city on market days.

INGREDIENTS

1/2 recipe Herb-Flavored Focaccia dough (page 26), completed through the first rising

1/4 small red (Spanish) onion, thinly sliced

1 1/2 teaspoons chopped fresh thyme

Extra-virgin olive oil for drizzling

2–3 tablespoons freshly grated Italian Parmesan cheese

METHOD FOR MAKING FOCACCIA WITH RED ONION

Lightly oil an 8-in/20-cm round cake pan or similar pan. Place the dough in the prepared pan and gently stretch it to the edges, pulling it from the center outward to achieve an even thickness. If the dough springs back toward the center and is difficult to work with, cover and set it aside to relax for 10 minutes, then continue coaxing the dough out to an even thickness. Cover with a kitchen towel and let rise until almost doubled in bulk and very soft and puffy, about 45 minutes.

Preheat an oven to 475°F/230°C/Gas Mark 6.

Using your fingertips, dimple the dough vigorously in several places, leaving indentations about 1/2 in/13 mm deep. Again cover the pan with a towel and let rise for 20 minutes longer.

Arrange the onion and thyme evenly over the risen dough. Drizzle the top with olive oil, then sprinkle on the Parmesan. Bake until golden brown and cooked through, 15–18 minutes. Transfer the pan to a rack and let stand until the focaccia is barely warm, about 10 minutes, then serve.

Makes one 8-in/20-cm focaccia
Preparation/Cooking time just over 2 hours

About Thyme

Thyme is part of a group of fragrant, shrubby mint plants native to the Mediterranean. Thyme has a sharp flavor that makes it a popular seasoning for chowders, meats, stuffings and sauces. Its appeal is indicated by the fact that it is always one of the herbs included in a traditional bouquet garni.

Throughout history, thyme has not only been used for culinary purposes: the ancient Egyptians embalmed with it; the ancient Greeks bathed in it and burned it in their temples. Today, thyme continues to be used for medicinal purposes—just as it has been used for hundreds of years. Thyme is found in preparations of cough medicines and mouthwashes. Its essential oil, thymol, helps with the digestion of fatty foods.

Perhaps most memorably of all, the delicious French liqueur Benedictine utilizes this wonderfully aromatic herb. (The Benedictine order of monks was founded in Italy sometime around AD 530).

Focaccia with Pesto and Potatoes

Potatoes and bread have a satisfying affinity for each other. A garlicky pesto sauce adds a luscious spark to this focaccia, perfect for lunch paired with a salad of baby greens. Although covered with potato slices, the pesto bubbles up during baking to contribute its special beauty to the finished round.

INGREDIENTS

1/2 recipe Herb-Flavored Focaccia dough (page 26), completed through the first rising

2 tablespoons olive oil

1/2 small yellow onion, thinly sliced

2–3 tablespoons Genovese Pesto (page 40)

1 very small russet or golden-fleshed potato, unpeeled, sliced paper-thin

2 tablespoons pine nuts

2 tablespoons freshly grated Italian Parmesan cheese

METHOD FOR MAKING FOCACCIA WITH PESTO AND POTATOES

Lightly oil an 8-in/20-cm round cake pan or similar pan. Place the dough in the prepared pan and gently stretch it to the edges, pulling it from the center outward to achieve an even thickness. If the dough springs back toward the center and is difficult to work with, cover and set it aside to relax for 10 minutes, then continue coaxing the dough out to an even thickness. Cover with a kitchen towel and let rise until almost doubled in bulk and very soft and puffy, about 45 minutes.

Preheat an oven to 475°F/230°C/Gas Mark 6.

Using your fingertips, dimple the dough vigorously in several places, leaving indentations about 1/2 in/13 mm deep. Again cover the pan with a towel and let the dough rise for 20 minutes longer.

While the dough is rising, in a small frying pan over medium-low heat, warm the olive oil. Add the onion and sauté until tender and golden, about 6 minutes. Remove from the heat and let cool.

Native to South America, the potato has become one of the most popular vegetables in the world.

Using the back of a spoon, spread the pesto evenly over the dough, using the larger amount if you want the finished focaccia to have a fuller pesto flavor. Arrange the potato slices in concentric circles atop the pesto, leaving gaps between the circles. Top evenly with the sautéed onion and the pine nuts. Scatter the Parmesan over the surface, including around the rim. Bake until golden brown and cooked through, 15–18 minutes. Transfer the pan to a rack and let stand until the focaccia is barely warm, about 10 minutes, then serve.

Makes one 8-in/20-cm focaccia
Preparation/Cooking time 2 hours

The aromas and flavors of garlicky pesto, potatoes and Parmesan combine well atop this delicious focaccia.

Porcini and Prosciutto Focaccia

Porcini mushrooms are eaten in Italy both fresh and dried, their flavor intensifying when dried. The combination of porcini, sun-dried tomatoes and prosciutto makes for an intensely tasty focaccia.

INGREDIENTS

1/2 oz/15 g dried porcini mushrooms

1 round Herb-Flavored Focaccia (page 26)

1/2 cup/4 fl oz/125 ml Sun-Dried Tomato Sauce (page 36)

2 slices prosciutto

1/4 cup/1 oz/30g grated mozzarella cheese

METHOD FOR MAKING PORCINI AND PROSCIUTTO FOCACCIA

Soak the porcini in water or stock to cover for 2 hours. Drain thoroughly and slice any large pieces.

Place a pizza brick, unglazed terracotta tile or baking sheet in the oven. Preheat oven to 450°F/220°C/Gas Mark 6.

Place the focaccia on the heated brick, tile or baking sheet. Spread the tomato sauce over the surface and then top with the mushrooms, prosciutto and mozzarella.

Bake for 15 minutes, or until the pizza is golden on the edges and crisp underneath.

Makes one 8-in/20-cm focaccia
Preparation/Cooking time just under 2½ hours

Seared Halibut Sandwich with Roasted Red Bell Pepper and Arugula

The American love of substantial sandwiches meets traditional Italian flavors in this panino. It is the type of lunch fare found at many of the new and stylish American pizzerias.

INGREDIENTS

1/2 red bell pepper (capsicum)

1/4 lb/125 g halibut fillet

1 tablespoon olive oil

Salt and freshly ground pepper

2 tablespoons mayonnaise

1 teaspoon chopped fresh thyme

1/2 teaspoon Dijon mustard

1 round Focaccia with Red Onion (page 218)

1/2 cup (1/2 oz/15 g) loosely packed arugula (rocket) leaves

2 thin slices red (Spanish) onion

Juice of 1/2 lemon

Preheat a broiler (griller) or oven to 450°F/220°C/ Gas Mark 6. Remove the seeds and ribs from the bell pepper (capsicum) half and place, cut side down, on a baking sheet. Place in the broiler or oven and broil (grill) or bake until the skin is charred and blistered. Alternatively, using tongs or a fork, hold the bell pepper half over a gas flame until charred and blistered. Immediately place the pepper half in a bowl and cover tightly with plastic wrap. Let steam until cool, about 15 minutes. Using your fingers, peel off the charred skin. Cut lengthwise into narrow strips. Set aside.

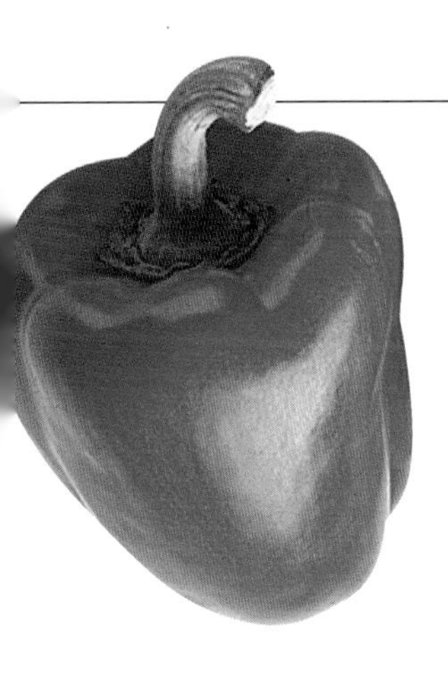

Preheat a gas grill or a ridged stove-top griddle on high, or place a heavy frying pan (preferably cast iron) over medium-high heat until very hot. Brush the halibut fillet with the olive oil and season to taste with salt and pepper. Add the fish to the hot grill, griddle or frying pan and cook, turning once, until nicely browned on both sides and opaque at the center, about 3 minutes on each side depending upon thickness.

While the fish cooks, in a bowl whisk the mayonnaise, thyme and mustard until blended.

Slice the focaccia in half horizontally. Cut the halibut into slices 1/2 in/13 mm thick. Spread the mustard mayonnaise on the cut sides of the focaccia. Distribute the arugula (rocket) evenly over the bottom of the focaccia. Top evenly with the sliced halibut and then with the bell pepper (capsicum) strips and onion slices. Sprinkle with the lemon juice and salt and pepper to taste. Place the other half of the focaccia on top, cut side down, and press down firmly with the palm of your hand. Cut the panino in half or in quarters for easier eating and serve.

Makes one sandwich, cut in half to serve 2
Preparation/Cooking time
45 minutes

Eggplant, Tomato and Mozzarella Sandwich

Here, the traditional ingredients for eggplant (aubergine) parmigiana are used to make a luscious panino. For a lighter version, grill rather than sauté the eggplant. The sandwich is delicious made while the eggplant is still warm.

INGREDIENTS

1 Asian (slender) eggplant (aubergine)

2 tablespoons olive oil

1 round Focaccia with Coarse Salt (page 202) or Focaccia with Red Onion (page 218)

1 tomato, sliced

2 thin slices Vidalia onion or other sweet onion

3 oz/90 g fresh mozzarella cheese, sliced

3 or 4 fresh basil leaves

Salt and freshly ground pepper

Extra-virgin olive oil for drizzling

2 tablespoons freshly grated Italian Parmesan cheese

METHOD FOR MAKING EGGPLANT, TOMATO AND MOZZARELLA SANDWICH

Trim the ends from the eggplant (aubergine) and thinly slice crosswise. Discard the end slices that are covered on one side with skin. In a frying pan over medium heat, warm the olive oil. Add the eggplant and cook, turning once, until tender and golden, 5–7 minutes. Using a slotted spoon, transfer to paper towels to drain.

Slice the focaccia in half horizontally. Arrange the eggplant (aubergine) slices on the bottom half. Top with the tomato, onion, mozzarella and basil. Season to taste with salt and pepper. Drizzle with olive oil and sprinkle with Parmesan. Place the other half of the focaccia on top, cut side down, and press down firmly with the palm of your hand. Cut the panino in half for easier eating and serve.

Makes one sandwich, cut in half to serve 2
Preparation/Cooking time 20 minutes

The extra flavor gained from choosing a focaccia with coarse salt or red onion adds to the enjoyment of the delicious ingredients.

Focaccia with Baked Ricotta

Ricotta is an Italian fresh cheese that is largely made from whey and has a slightly sweet flavor. Here, baked ricotta is combined with prosciutto, mushrooms, sun-dried tomatoes and Jarlsberg cheese to produce a delicious focaccia.

INGREDIENTS

1 lb/500 g ricotta cheese

6 tablespoons olive oil

Salt

Freshly ground black pepper

1 teaspoon paprika

2 onions, thinly sliced

2 rounds Herb-Flavored Focaccia (page 26)

8 slices prosciutto

8 oz/250 g mushrooms, sliced

12 sun-dried tomatoes

4 slices Jarlsberg cheese

Basil sprigs for garnish (optional)

METHOD FOR MAKING FOCCACIA WITH BAKED RICOTTA

Preheat oven to 350°F/180°C/Gas Mark 4.

Place ricotta on an oiled baking dish. Drizzle with 2 tablespoons of the olive oil, salt, pepper and paprika. Place in the oven and bake for 25–30 minutes.

Heat two tablespoons of the oil in a large pan, add onions and cook until soft. Set aside in a warm place.

Divide the focaccia into four equal pieces, slice horizontally in half and brush each side with a little of the remaining oil. Assemble by piling all the ingredients onto one side, ending with Jarlsberg cheese.

Place under a preheated broiler (griller) and broil (grill) until cheese melts. Top with the other half and serve immediately, garnished with basil if desired.

Makes two 8-in/20-cm focaccia, cut in half to serve 4
Preparation/Cooking time 45 minutes

Paprika is made of dried and powdered red bell peppers (capsicums).

Grilled Vegetable Focaccia with Rosemary Oil

This wholesome focaccia is wonderful served hot from the grill, but is also excellent eaten cold, making it an ideal inclusion in a patio menu.

INGREDIENTS

ROSEMARY OIL

1 1/2 cups/12 fl oz/375 ml extra-virgin olive oil

3 cloves garlic

5 fresh rosemary sprigs

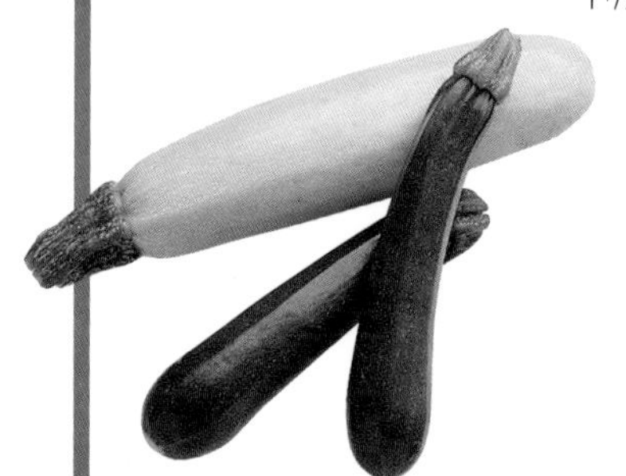

GRILLED VEGETABLES

1 red bell pepper (capsicum)

4 thin slices fennel, cut through the stem end

4 slices eggplant (aubergine), cut crosswise

1 zucchini (courgette), thinly sliced lengthwise

12 asparagus spears, tough ends removed

1/2 teaspoon salt

1/2 teaspoon freshly ground black pepper

1 teaspoon chopped fresh thyme

1 teaspoon finely chopped garlic

1 fresh portobello mushroom, brushed clean

4 slices red (Spanish) onion

2 rounds Herb-Flavored Focaccia (page 26)

1 tablespoon balsamic vinegar

1 1/2 cups/1 1/2 oz/45 g lightly packed inner yellow frisée leaves

METHOD FOR MAKING GRILLED VEGETABLE FOCCACIA WITH ROSEMARY OIL

To make the rosemary oil, in a small saucepan over a low heat, combine the oil, garlic cloves and three of the rosemary sprigs and heat until the oil is too hot to touch comfortably, about 5 minutes. Remove from the heat and discard the rosemary sprigs Add the remaining two rosemary sprigs to the oil and set aside.

To prepare the grilled vegetables, prepare a fire in a charcoal grill using hardwood charcoal such as mesquite or hickory.

While the coals are still glowing red, place the bell pepper (capsicum) on the grill rack and grill, turning as necessary until charred on all sides. Remove and let cool for 5 mintues in a sealed plastic bag, then, using your fingers or a small knife, peel off the charred skin. Cut in half lengthwise and remove the seeds and ribs. Cut each half in half again. Set aside.

Bring a saucepan three-fourths full of water to the boil. Add the fennel, boil for 1 minute and drain. In a large bowl, toss together the fennel, eggplant (aubergine), zucchini (courgette), asparagus, salt, pepper, thyme and garlic. Drizzle on just enough of the rosemary oil to coat everything lightly and toss again.

Brush the mushroom and the onion slices with some of the remaining rosemary oil.

When the coals have burned down to a gray ash, place all the vegetables on the grill rack and cook until they begin to appear translucent. Turn the vegetables as needed and move them around on the grill to prevent burning. The fennel and eggplant (aubergine) will take 3 minutes on each side; the mushroom 2–3 minutes on each side; the asparagus and zucchini (courgette) about 2 minutes on each side.

To assemble the sandwiches, split the focaccias in half horizontally. Brush the cut sides lightly with the remaining rosemary oil and place, cut sides down, over the coals to toastt lightly. Place the bottoms, cut sides up, on four plates. Divide the grilled vegetables evenly among the focaccia bottoms. Cut the mushroom into four slices and place a mushroom slice and a piece of roasted bell pepper atop each stack of vegetables. Drizzle the balsamic vinegar evenly over the tops, then cover with equal amounts of the frisée and finally the focaccia tops.

Makes two 8-in/20-cm rounds, cut in half to serve 4
Preparation/Cooking time 2 hours

MINI PIZZAS AND DIFFERENT BASES

Mini Pizzas

The myriad ways to make pizza have led to its becoming one of the world's best-loved meals—there's a way to make the dough and to top it to suit just about everyone. From yeast-free and wholewheat bases to vegetarian, combined with seafood and other delicious ingredients for the topping, the pizza probably stands as one of the most diverse dishes to be made in any country, to be on the menu of any restaurant or to be served in any home.

The evolution of the pizza from its humble beginnings in Naples over a century ago still continues, with diversity as its key factor. A large disk of dough may be the traditional base and shape, but there are other ways pizza can be served. This section takes you one step further from the assorted pizza base recipes given at the start of this book,to reveal other ways you can create the base: with a delicious short pastry, puff pastry, crusty Italian bread, pita or lavash bread, tortillas, tostadas and tacos.

There are mini pizzas, or pizzettas, that are perfect as finger food at a party, or as special treats served cold at a picnic. Top them with stringy mozzarella cheese and your children's favorite foods for a kids' party, or with smoked salmon, marscapone and chives to create more sophisticated fare for a formal outdoors get-together.

This section also presents many other easy and tempting recipes, such as tomato bruschetta, with herbed tomatoes served on Italian toasts; tomatoes and goat cheese on squares of puff pastry; Greek-style pizza on pita bread; an Italian variety of pizza with pita; mussel-filled tostadas; beef tacos; and even a delicious diet pizza served on wholewheat pita. The wonderful variety of ways to make your "pizza"—to utilize traditional pizza ingredients in new ways and to bring some new ingredients into the pizza parlor—open up new ways to enjoy an old favorite.

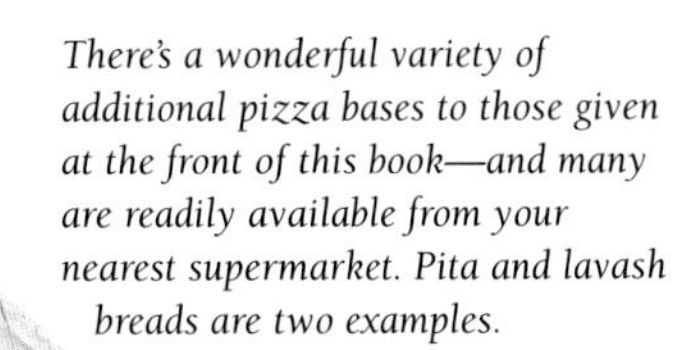

There's a wonderful variety of additional pizza bases to those given at the front of this book—and many are readily available from your nearest supermarket. Pita and lavash breads are two examples.

Blue Cheese Pita Pizza

This is one of the simplest of pizzas, and one of the tastiest. The delicious flavor of a rich blue cheese, such as Roquefort, combined with the taste and texture of the walnuts is a winning combination.

INGREDIENTS

1 large (9½ in/24 cm) pita or lavash bread

½ cup/4 fl oz/125 ml Basic Tomato Sauce (page 34)

3½ oz/100 g blue cheese, such as Roquefort, crumbled

¼ cup/1 oz/30 g walnut pieces

Preheat oven to 450°F/220°C/Gas Mark 6.

Place a pita or lavash bread on a baking sheet, spread the tomato sauce over the surface and then top with the crumbled cheese and the walnuts.

Bake for 15 minutes, or until the pizza is golden on the edges and crisp underneath.

Makes one large pita or lavash bread
Preparation/Cooking time 30 minutes

Choose the rich and creamy Roquefort with its definite piquant aftertaste, or the equally strong Gorgonzola to top this pizza. Milder blue cheeses are also available, and will give an equally delicious result.

Pizza Crusts

Here is a variety of tasty pizza crusts you can offer at your next party or prior to serving your next special dinner. They're light, not too filling and whet the appetite for what's to come.

INGREDIENTS

Select from any of the plain pizza-base recipes given at the front of this book (pages 16 to 25).

GARLIC CRUSTS

1 tablespoon olive oil

3 cloves garlic, chopped

CHILI CRUSTS

1 tablespoon olive oil

2 teaspoons chopped chili

PESTO CRUSTS

1/4 cup/2 oz/60 g Pesto (page 43)

HERB CRUSTS

1 tablespoon olive oil

2 teaspoons chopped mixed herbs

METHOD FOR MAKING PIZZA CRUSTS

Place a pizza brick, unglazed terracotta tile or baking sheet in the oven. Preheat oven to 450°F/220°C/Gas Mark 6.

On a floured surface, press out the pizza dough using your fingertips into a 10-in/25-cm circle (always pressing from the center of the dough to the outside).

Place the pizza dough on the heated brick, tile or baking sheet. Mix together your chosen combination of ingredients and spread the mixture over the pizza base.

Bake for 15 minutes, or until the pizza is golden on the edges and crisp underneath.

Serve the crusts, cut into wedges, with a dip or by themselves. This is a good way to use up any leftover pizza dough.

Makes one 10-in/25-cm pizza
Preparation/Cooking time 30 minutes

Diet Mini Pizzas

Topped with an abundance of fresh vegetables, these diet pizzas are a feast for the eyes and tastebuds, with their variety of colors, tastes and textures. They're served on a wholewheat pita with low-fat ricotta, so you can now safely indulge!

INGREDIENTS

1/4 cup/1 oz/30 g julienned fresh baby corn

1/2 cup/1 1/2 oz/45 g julienned carrots

1/4 cup/1 oz/30 g julienned snow peas (mangetout)

1/4 cup/1 oz/30 g julienned zucchini (courgette)

1/4 cup/1 oz/30 g julienned yellow bell pepper (capsicum)

1 tablespoon olive oil

8 individual wholewheat pita breads

1/2 cup/4 fl oz/125 ml Basic Tomato Sauce (page 34)

3 1/2 oz/100 g low-fat ricotta cheese

METHOD FOR MAKING DIET MINI PIZZAS

Preheat oven to 400°F/200°C/Gas Mark 5.

Heat the olive oil in a small frying pan over medium heat. Add all of the vegetables and sauté until just tender, about 5 minutes.

Arrange the pita breads on a baking sheet. Top each with some of the tomato sauce, then a little of the cheese. Divide the vegetables among the pita breads and arrange on top.

Bake for 10–15 minutes, or until heated through.

Makes eight individual pita breads (to serve four)
Preparation/Cooking time 25 minutes

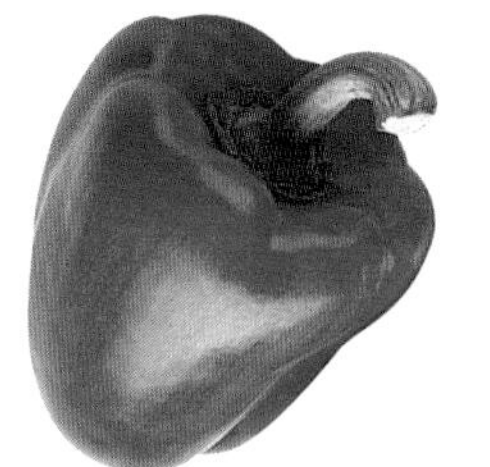

Smoked Salmon and Mascarpone Pizzettas

These simple and totally delicious little pizzas are served cold—making them a perfect addition to any picnic basket or other outdoor summer gathering.

INGREDIENTS

Select from any of the plain pizza-base recipes (from pages 16 to 25), made into 6 mini bases

1 cup/7 oz/220 g mascarpone cheese, at room temperature

10 slices smoked salmon

1/4 cup chopped chives

2 tablespoons extra-virgin olive oil

Freshly ground black pepper

METHOD FOR MAKING SMOKED SALMON AND MASCARPONE PIZZETTAS

Spread each pizzetta base with 2–3 tablespoons of mascarpone.

Divide salmon into equal portions and arrange over mascarpone.

Sprinkle with chives and drizzle with oil. Sprinkle with pepper and serve.

Serves 6
Preparation time 5 minutes

You'll find it very difficult to stop at just one of these little pizzettas! Creamy soft mascarpone, usually served with desserts, provides the perfect contrast to the savory flavor of the smoked salmon.

Spinach and Pine Nut Pizzettas

Pine nuts are widely used in Italy, their delicious and delicate flavor making them a perfect choice for pizzas, salads and other meals.

INGREDIENTS

8 leaves spinach, stems removed

1 tablespoon water

1 tablespoon olive oil

6 garlic cloves, halved

1/3 cup/1 3/4 oz/50 g pine nuts

2 oz/60 g Parmesan cheese, shaved

Select from any of the plain pizza-base recipes (from pages 16 to 25), made into 6 mini bases

METHOD FOR MAKING SPINACH AND PINE NUT PIZZETTAS

Preheat oven to 350°F/180°C/ Gas Mark 4.

Place the spinach in a saucepan Add the water and cook, covered, for 5 minutes, or until wilted. Drain and squeeze out excess water.

Heat the oil in a pan, add the garlic halves and fry until golden.

Toast the pine nuts on a baking sheet in the oven for 4 minutes.

Assemble pizzettas by layering ingredients on the warm bases. Place under a broiler (griller) just to melt the Parmesan.

Makes six pizzettas
Preparation/Cooking time
25 minutes

Sun-Dried Tomato, Mushroom and Bell Pepper Pizzettas

These pizzettas once again combine typically Italian ingredients to bring you a taste to remember.

INGREDIENTS

12 sun-dried tomatoes

2 tablespoons olive oil

2 garlic cloves, finely chopped

6 mushrooms, sliced

Select from any of the plain pizza-base recipes (from pages 16 to 25), made into 6 mini bases

1 1/2 cups/12 fl oz/375 ml Basic Tomato Sauce (page 34)

1 bell pepper, roasted, seeded and peeled

1/2 cup/60 g/2 oz grated Parmesan cheese

Freshly ground black pepper

METHOD FOR MAKING TOMATO, MUSHROOM AND BELL PEPPER PIZZETTAS

Chop tomatoes into strips and set aside. Heat oil in a pan (including any extra oil from the sun-dried tomatoes), add garlic and mushrooms and cook until mushrooms are tender.

Top pizzetta bases with the tomato sauce and then the rest of the ingredients, ending with the Parmesan and pepper.

Place under a broiler (griller) to melt Parmesan, then serve.

Makes six pizzettas
Preparation/Cooking time
20 minutes

With their topping of sun-dried tomatoes, roasted peppers, Parmesan and garlic, these pizzettas offer some of the classic flavors of Italy.

Coppa Pizza

Coppa is a type of cured pork which is very popular in Italy. This pizza also utilizes another cured meat, pancetta, which possesses a more delicate texture and taste than coppa.

INGREDIENTS

1 large (9½ in/24 cm) pita bread

½ cup/4 fl oz/125 ml Basic Tomato Sauce (page 34)

3½ oz/100 g coppa or cooked smoked bacon or ham, thinly sliced

2 oz/60 g pancetta or salami, thinly sliced

1½ oz/45 g mozzarella cheese, thinly sliced

4 cherry tomatoes, halved

1 tablespoon pine nuts

1 teaspoon rosemary leaves

2 teaspoons black olive paste (tapenade)

METHOD FOR MAKING COPPA PIZZA

Preheat oven to 450°F/220°C/Gas Mark 6.

Place the pita bread on a baking sheet. Spoon the tomato sauce over the pita bread. Arrange the coppa and pancetta on top of the sauce. Top with the mozzarella, tomato halves, pine nuts and rosemary. Dot the olive paste around the pizza.

Bake for 10 minutes or until the cheese is melted.

Makes one large pita bread
Preparation/Cooking time 20 minutes

It's amazing how simple to prepare and, at the same time, how tasty a pizza can be. This one, utilizing a pita base and ingredients that require hardly any preparation, is quick, easy and delicious.

Greek-Style Pita Bread Pizza

In this recipe, some typically Greek ingredients provide an interesting variety of topping for a pizza.

INGREDIENTS

1 large (9-inch/22-cm) pita bread

1 tablespoon Pesto (page 42)

1 tablespoon black olive paste (tapenade)

3 1/2 oz/100 g feta cheese, cut into 1/4-in/6-mm cubes

3/4 oz/20 g pitted Kalamata olives

METHOD FOR MAKING GREEK-STYLE PITA BREAD PIZZA

Preheat oven to 400°F/200°C/ Gas Mark 5.

Place the pita bread on a baking sheet. Spread the pesto and olive paste over the bread. Arrange the cheese and olives on top.

Bake for 10 minutes, or until crisp.

Makes one large pita bread
Preparation/Cooking time
15 minutes

This pizza's tangy combination of ingredients—pesto, olive paste, olives and feta—gives it a mouthwatering burst of flavor.

Pissaladière

Tomatoes have been added to this version of the classic Provençal onion-and-anchovy tart. It is similar to a pizza but has a short pastry base.

INGREDIENTS

PASTRY

2 cups/8 oz/250 g all-purpose (plain) flour

10 tablespoons/5 oz/155 g unsalted butter

2 tablespoons ice water

FILLING

2 tablespoons olive oil

8 white onions, finely chopped

2 cloves garlic, chopped

5 ripe tomatoes (about 1 1/3 lb/ 615 g), peeled, seeded and finely chopped

Freshly ground pepper

3 oz/90 g anchovies in oil, drained

3/4 cup/3 1/2 oz/100 g Niçoise or Kalamata olives (optional)

METHOD FOR MAKING PISSALADIÈRE

To make the pastry, mix the flour and butter in a food processor until it resembles coarse meal. Add the water and process until the mixture forms a ball. Wrap in plastic wrap and refrigerate for 30 minutes.

For the filling, heat the oil in a pan and cook the onions and garlic over medium heat for approximately 5 minutes or until soft, stirring regularly. Add the tomatoes and continue cooking for 20 minutes or until the liquid is almost completely reduced and the mixture resembles a thick pulp. Let cool and season with pepper to taste.

Preheat the oven to 400°F/200°C/Gas Mark 5. Roll out the pastry to fit a shallow 10½-in/27-cm tart pan and transfer the pastry to the pan. Add the filling and arrange the anchovies and olives on top. Cook for 40 minutes or until the pastry is golden brown. Serve hot or at room temperature.

Serves 6
Preparation/Cooking time 1½ hours

The salty taste of the anchovies and olives creates a pizza with a strong and distinctive flavor.

About Tomatoes

Tomatoes are one of the most popularly eaten fruits in the world. The tomato's appearance—most often a clear, bright and shiny red—makes it appealing to look at, and once you take a bite into its firm flesh, you discover a very special taste ... one you are never likely to tire of. Raw or cooked, as tomato sauce, tomato soup, tomato juice, in sandwiches and salads, prepared as sun-dried or semi-dried tomatoes, and as a topping for pizzas, it seems there is almost no end to how you can enjoy the tomato.

The earliest tomatoes were gathered in the wild by the Indian people of the Andes of South America. From there the tomato was brought to Europe in the 1500s by the Spanish—and the rest, as they say, is history. It was another 200 years, however, before the humble tomato gained its strong position in the cuisines of Europe. The Italians were the first to commonly add tomato to their dishes, the remaining countries following suit after the quelling of initial scares brought about by the tomato's link to its poisonous relatives, such as deadly nightshade.

The best tomatoes are vine ripened, providing the maximum flavor.

Tomato Mini Pizzas

These little pizzas can be prepared well in advance and cooked just before serving. They are best eaten hot from the oven or warm, and make an ideal finger food served with drinks.

INGREDIENTS

2 sheets prepared puff pastry, thawed

Olive oil, for brushing

7 oz/220 g goat cheese, sliced

1 cup/8 oz/250 g cherry tomatoes, finely sliced

1 cup/8 oz/250 g yellow pear (teardrop) tomatoes, finely sliced

Fresh oregano sprigs

Freshly ground black pepper

METHOD FOR MAKING TOMATO MINI PIZZAS

Preheat the oven to 400°F/ 200°C/Gas Mark 5.

Using a cookie or ravioli cutter, cut the pastry into small rounds or squares. Place on a large cookie sheet covered with greased baking paper.

Brush each piece with oil and top with a slice of goat cheese. Arrange the cherry tomatoes on one half of the pastry rounds, and the yellow pear tomatoes on the other half. Brush again with oil and sprinkle with oregano and black pepper.

Bake for 12–15 minutes until pastry is golden brown.

Makes about 25 mini pizzas **Preparation/Cooking time** 25 minutes

Tomato Bruschetta

Slices of French or Italian bread make an easy base for a pizza topping. These bruschetta can be served as an appetizer, an antipasto or a light luncheon dish. Use the best tomatoes available for this wonderfully simple dish.

INGREDIENTS

3 large tomatoes (about 15 oz/470 g), peeled, seeded and finely diced

Salt

1/2 cup/1 oz/30 g fresh basil, finely shredded

1/2 cup/1 oz/30 g finely chopped flat-leaf (Italian) parsley

1/3 cup/2 1/2 fl oz/80 ml extra-virgin olive oil

Dash balsamic vinegar

Salt and freshly ground black pepper

1 loaf Italian bread, cut into 12 slices

1/2 cup/4 fl oz/125 ml olive oil

2 cloves garlic, peeled and halved

METHOD FOR MAKING TOMATO BRUSCHETTA

Sprinkle the tomatoes with salt and allow them to drain in a colander for 1 hour. Rinse off the salt and pat dry. In a bowl, combine the basil, parsley, oil and vinegar. Mix well and season with salt and pepper to taste. Add the drained tomatoes.

Toast the bread under a broiler (griller) and brush the slices generously with the olive oil. Rub each slice with garlic, spoon on the tomato mixture, and serve immediately.

Makes 12 slices (2 per person)
Preparation/Cooking time 1 hour 15 minutes

For the best flavor, use fresh basil and parsley and vine-ripened tomatoes.

Thai Shrimp Pizza

The wonderful flavors of Thai food include one of the oldest known herbs—cilantro. However, cilantro is native to the Mediterranean, and is also a popular herb in Italian cuisine.

INGREDIENTS

1 large (10 x 8-in/25 x 20-cm) pita or lavash bread

1–2 tablespoons Thai sweet chili sauce

1–2 teaspoons chopped fresh cilantro (coriander/Chinese parsley)

6½ oz/185 g cooked and peeled large shrimp (king prawns)

⅔ cup/2½ oz/75 g chopped shallots

1 tablespoon raw, unsalted peanuts

A few strips of fresh or desiccated coconut

METHOD FOR MAKING THAI SHRIMP PIZZA

Preheat oven to 400°F/200°C/ Gas Mark 5.

Place the pita or lavash bread on a baking sheet.

Brush the bread with the Thai sweet chili sauce. Sprinkle with the chopped cilantro. Top with the shrimp, shallots, peanuts and coconut strips.

Bake for 3–5 minutes, or until the pizza is heated through. Garnish with a little extra coriander if desired.

Makes one large pita or lavash bread
Preparation/Cooking time
15 minutes

A touch of coconut adds a fresh and interesting flavor to this pizza.

Quick Pita Bread Pizza

Many pizza lovers enjoy the taste of pineapple on their creations, adding an exotic flavor to even the most traditional of pizzas.

INGREDIENTS

2 large white pita bread pockets (about 8 in/20 cm in diameter)

1/4 cup/2 fl oz/60 ml store-bought pasta sauce or Basic Tomato Sauce (page 34)

6 thick slices spicy salami, shredded

2 thick slices cooked ham, finely diced or ground (minced)

2 tablespoons sliced, stuffed green olives

3 tablespoons diced green bell pepper

3 tablespoons drained, crushed or finely diced canned pineapple

1/2 cup/2 1/2 oz/75 g grated mozzarella or other melting cheese

2 teaspoons dried Italian or Provençal mixed herbs

METHOD FOR MAKING QUICK PITA BREAD PIZZA

Place the pita breads on a baking sheet and spread with the pasta sauce. Mix the salami and ham together and spread evenly over. Top with the remaining ingredients, scattering the cheese on top.

Heat under a hot broiler (griller) until the cheese melts—about 4 minutes. Serve immediately.

Makes two large pita breads
Preparation/Cooking time
15 minutes

Pita and lavash bread are low in fat and make a healthy base for your pizza topping.

Anchovy Toasts

In Spain, anchovy toasts are served as a snack with apéritifs. For a true indulgence, try them with a lightly chilled fino sherry.

INGREDIENTS

4 slices country-style bread, cut 1/2 in/1 cm thick

Olive oil

1 large, very ripe tomato

48 oil-packed anchovy fillets

Lightly toast the bread, then brush with olive oil. Cut the tomato in halves and rub over one surface of the bread to coat with the tomato juice and pulp. Arrange 12 drained anchovy fillets diagonally on each piece of toast. Cut in halves and serve at once.

Makes four serves **Preparation time** 10 minutes

Mussel Ceviche Tostadas

Tostadas take their name from their bases of toasted—that is, crisply fried—tortillas. They are variously topped with beans, lettuce, cheeses and, often, poultry or meat.

INGREDIENTS

3 lb/1.5 kg mussels in the shell

1 cup/8 fl oz/250 ml dry white wine

6 bay leaves

2 ripe tomatoes, seeded and diced

1 small red (Spanish) onion, diced

1 cup/5½ oz/170 g small Spanish green olives or other small green olives such as French picholines

3 tablespoons coarsely chopped fresh oregano

⅔ cup/5 fl oz/160 ml good-quality tomato juice

⅓ cup/2½ fl oz/80 ml fresh orange juice

⅓ cup/2½ fl oz/80 ml fresh lime juice

¼ cup/2 fl oz/60 ml fruity Spanish olive oil or other fruity olive oil

1 teaspoon salt

½ teaspoon freshly ground pepper

6–8 small corn tortillas, homemade (page 19) or purchased

Vegetable oil for frying

1 ripe avocado, pitted, peeled and mashed

METHOD FOR MAKING MUSSEL CEVICHE TOSTADAS

Scrub the mussels under cool running water and pull off and discard their beards. Discard any mussels that do not close to the touch.

In a large frying pan, combine the wine and bay leaves and bring to a boil. Add enough mussels to the pan to cover the bottom in a single layer; cover, reduce the heat to medium and cook until they open, 3–5 minutes. Using a slotted spoon, lift out the mussels and transfer to a bowl to cool. Cook the remaining mussels in batches in the same liquid, discarding any mussels that do not open. Reserve the cooking liquid for another use.

Remove the mussels from their shells and place them in a non-aluminum bowl. Add the tomatoes, onion, olives, oregano, tomato and citrus juices, olive oil, salt and pepper and stir gently to mix. Cover and refrigerate for 1–2 hours to allow the flavors to blend.

Meanwhile, pour oil to a depth of 1/2 in/13 mm in a small frying pan and heat to 375°F/190°C on a deep-frying thermometer. Working with one tortilla at a time and using tongs, slip the tortilla into the oil and fry, turning once, until crispy but not browned, about 1 minute on each side. Drain on paper towels while you fry the other tortillas.

To serve, place the tortillas on individual plates. Divide the ceviche evenly among the tortillas, spooning it on top. Place a dollop of mashed avocado on each and serve.

Makes 6–8 tortillas
Preparation/ Cooking time
up to 2 hours 15 minutes

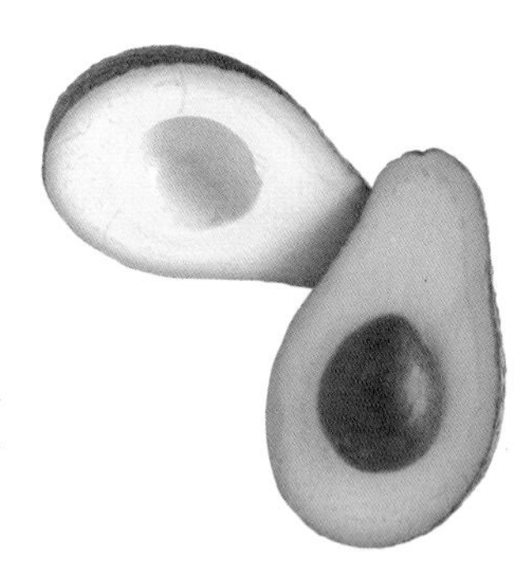

About Mussels

Surrounded by the azure blue waters of the Mediterranean, Italy is blessed with a resource that gives its cuisine the special and delicious taste of seafood. And mussels are one of the most popular additions to its seafood dishes. Found in sauces alla Marinara that are poured over fresh pasta and even atop the humble pizza, mussels have become a staple part of the seafood diet of Italy.

Mussels are edible mollusks, closely related to the clam. Both salt-water and freshwater varieties exist. Marine mussels are the variety enjoyed in so many dishes. They usually live in shallow waters along ocean coasts, and attach themselves to rocks or piers by producing strong, sticky threads made of protein. Freshwater mussels are only distantly related to marine mussels, and were once a major source of mother-of-pearl, a rainbow-colored material that lines their shells. Freshwater mussels are now scarce.

Fresh mussels should have closed shells which, upon cooking, open up. Do not attempt to eat mussels from shells which have not naturally opened upon cooking—they are probably stale.

Grilled Beef Tacos

In the beef-eating north of Mexico, taco stands usually feature some form of charcoal-grilled skirt steak. Offer an array of condiments, and let your guests be creative.

INGREDIENTS

QUICK SALSA

4 ripe plum (Roma) tomatoes, seeded and coarsely chopped

2 fresh serrano chili peppers, stemmed and coarsely chopped

3 tablespoons fresh lime juice

1 teaspoon salt

1/2 teaspoon freshly ground black pepper

GARNISHES

1/4 cup/1/3 oz/10 g coarsely chopped fresh cilantro (fresh coriander)

2 avocados, pitted, peeled and diced

2 tomatoes, seeded and diced

6 green (spring) onions, including the tender green tops, sliced on the diagonal

1/4 head white cabbage, shredded

1 1/2 lb/750 g trimmed skirt, flank or tri-tip (sirloin) steaks

Salt and freshly ground black pepper

2 cloves garlic, minced

2 tablespoons olive oil

Juice of 1 lime

18 small or 12 large corn tortillas, homemade (page 19) or purchased

METHOD FOR MAKING GRILLED BEEF TACOS

Prepare a fire in a charcoal grill.

To make the salsa, in a food processor fitted with the metal blade, combine the tomatoes, chilies, lime juice, salt and black pepper and purée until very smooth. Pour into a bowl and set aside. You should have about 1¼ cups/10 fl oz/300 ml. Prepare all the garnishes and place in separate bowls.

Ten minutes before the grill is ready, season the steaks evenly with salt and black pepper, rub with the garlic and olive oil and then drizzle evenly with the lime juice.

Just before grilling the steaks, warm the tortillas on the grill: Fill a shallow pan with water and, one at a time, briefly dip each tortilla in the water and immediately place on the grill rack. Grill for 30 seconds, then turn and grill for 30 seconds longer. Stack the tortillas as they come off the grill and wrap them in a damp towel and then in aluminum foil until serving. (They will keep warm for up to 30 minutes.)

When the fire is very hot, place the steaks on the grill rack about 3 in/7.5 cm from the coals and grill, turning once, until evenly browned on the outside but remaining pink in the center, 1–2 minutes per side.

Transfer the steaks to a cutting board and let rest for 3–5 minutes before slicing. Using a sharp knife, cut across the grain into slices ¼ in/6 mm thick. Serve immediately with the warmed tortillas, salsa and garnishes. Let diners assemble their own tacos at the table.

Makes up to 12 large tortillas (to serve six)
Preparation/Cooking time 45 minutes

The basic bread of Mexico is the tortilla. Its forms include the taco, a folded, fried tortilla filled with chopped ingredients; the enchilada, a rolled-up tortilla with a similar filling and covered with sauce; or the tostada, a tortilla deep-fried until it becomes crisp, and served with a topping of chopped ingredients.

Lamb Pizza

Open-faced meat pies like these are popular café food in Syria, Lebanon and Israel, as well as in Turkey. The dough is a cross between that used for an Italian pizza and Turkish *pide* bread. You can also shape it into smaller 4-in/10-cm pies. Add the chilies if you prefer a little heat.

INGREDIENTS

SPONGE

1 envelope/2 1/2 teaspoons active dry yeast

1 teaspoon sugar

1/2 cup/4 fl oz/125 ml lukewarm water (105°F/40°C)

1/2 cup/2 1/2 oz/75 g unbleached bread flour

DOUGH

4 1/2 cups/22 1/2 oz/675 g unbleached bread flour

2 teaspoons salt

2 tablespoons olive oil

1 1/2 cups/12 fl oz/375 ml lukewarm water (105°F/40°C)

LAMB FILLING

2 tablespoons olive oil

1 large onion, finely chopped

4 cloves garlic, minced

1 lb/500 g ground (minced) lamb

1½ cups/9 oz/280 g peeled, seeded and chopped tomatoes

½ cup/2 oz/60 g mild green chili peppers, minced (optional)

½ teaspoon ground allspice

1 teaspoon ground cinnamon

½ cup/½ oz/15 g chopped fresh flat-leaf (Italian) parsley

Salt and ground black pepper

¼ cup/1 oz/30 g pine nuts

Olive oil for brushing on pizzas

¼ cup/⅓ oz/10 g chopped fresh mint

pine nuts

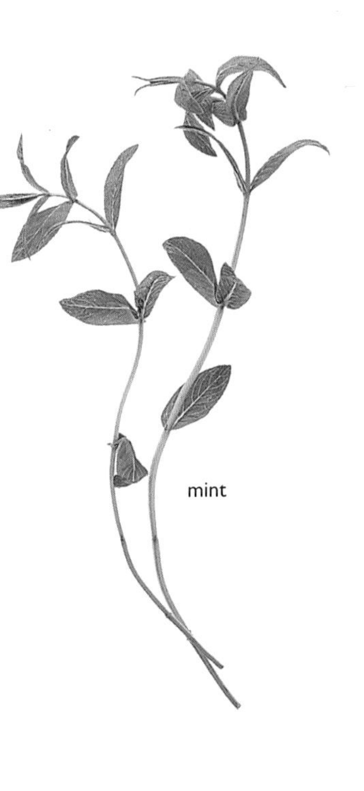
mint

METHOD FOR MAKING LAMB PIZZA

To make the sponge, in a small bowl, dissolve the yeast and sugar in the lukewarm water. Stir in the flour and let stand in a warm place until bubbly, about 5 minutes.

To make the dough in an electric stand mixer, place the flour in the bowl of the mixer and add the sponge, salt, olive oil and lukewarm water. Using the paddle attachment, mix on low speed to combine. Then attach the dough hook and beat on medium speed until the dough is smooth, elastic and pulls away cleanly from the bowl sides, 5–6 minutes.

To make the dough by hand, place the flour in a large bowl and add the sponge, salt, olive oil and lukewarm water. Stir until a soft dough forms, then turn out onto a lightly floured work surface and knead until smooth and elastic, about 10–12 minutes.

Shape the dough into a ball, place in an oiled bowl and turn to coat evenly. Cover the bowl with plastic wrap and let rise in a warm place until doubled, 45–60 minutes.

Meanwhile, make the lamb filling: In a large frying pan over medium heat, warm the olive oil. Add the onion and sauté until tender, about 10 minutes. Add the garlic and lamb, raise the heat to high and sauté until it begins to brown, 5–8 minutes. Add the tomatoes, chilies (if using), allspice and cinnamon and cook uncovered, stirring occasionally, for about 30 minutes. The mixture should be very thick. Stir in half of the parsley and season to taste with salt and pepper. Let cool.

Meanwhile, turn out the dough onto a lightly floured work surface and knead briefly. Divide into 12 equal portions and form each portion into a ball. Place the balls on the work surface, cover with a kitchen towel and let rest for 30 minutes.

Preheat an oven to 350°F/180°C/Gas Mark 4. Spread the pine nuts in a small pan and toast in the oven until fragrant, 6–8 minutes. Let cool.

Raise the oven temperature to 500°F/240°C/Gas Mark 7. Roll out each ball of dough into a round 6 in/15 cm in diameter. Place the rounds, spaced well apart, on baking sheets. Brush lightly with olive oil and then divide the filling evenly among them, leaving a 1/2-in/12-mm border uncovered. Sprinkle evenly with the pine nuts.

Bake until the crust is golden, about 6 minutes. Sprinkle with the remaining parsley and the mint and serve hot.

Makes Twelve 6-in/15-cm pizzas
Preparation/Cooking time
just over 2 hours

SWEET PIZZAS

Sweet Pizzas

After delighting your family and friends with your inventive and delicious savory pizzas, why not finish off the meal with yet another one of your novel creations?

Sweet pizzas combine two of the most popular meals ever enjoyed—pizza and dessert! Though very simple to prepare, this presentation of two old favorites demonstrates the interest and fun that can be had with food … and the results are, quite simply, delicious.

Present your guests not only with excellent food, tempting aromas, mouth-watering tastes and stunning presentation, but also with the challenge of trying, yet again, something new. Once more, pizza's versatility—its place as an inspiration for invention—is proven.

The following section gives you some wonderful ideas on just how you can create a delicious sweet pizza. It shows you how you can use a traditional pizza base, such as Neapolitan, or make up a sweet pizza dough or even a biscuit- or scone-like dough, to use as the foundation for your own sweet pizza.

The toppings presented here include the delicious flavors of healthy fresh fruit. You can of course add your own favorite dessert foods to these toppings. Finish off these creations in your own inimitable style: a drizzle of warm raspberry or chocolate sauce, a scoop of ice cream or a sprinkle of crushed nuts where appropriate are just a few ideas.

Pizza is so appropriate for celebratory occasions—it provides a self-serve, casual way of entertaining a group or crowd. On such special occasions, why not make a birthday pizza for that pizza-fiend friend or child? After all, life should be full of delightful and memorable experiences.

Enjoy the fruits of the forest atop a pizza! The recipe for this delicious Berry Pizza appears on page 302.

Sweet Pizza with Fruit and Almonds

A pizzeria sometimes pairs standard dough with sweet toppings to create a rustic dessert. With this pizza, the intense heat of the hot pizza stone helps the ingredients to caramelize quickly, producing a homey dish that is creamy yet not too rich.

INGREDIENTS

Neapolitan Pizza Dough (page 22), completed through the second rising

All-purpose (plain) flour for dusting

1 cup/7 oz/220 g mascarpone cheese

2 teaspoons plus 2 tablespoons sugar

2 egg yolks

2 baking apples, such as Granny Smith or Gravenstein, halved, cored and thinly sliced

1 pear, halved, cored and thinly sliced

2 tablespoons coarsely chopped almonds

METHOD FOR MAKING SWEET PIZZA WITH FRUIT AND ALMONDS

Place a pizza brick, unglazed terracotta tile or baking sheet on the lowest rack of an oven. Preheat to 475°F/230°C/Gas Mark 6.

Cut each ball of dough into 2 equal pieces so that you have 4 balls. One at a time, place the balls on a lightly floured work surface and flatten slightly. Sprinkle a little flour on the top of the dough and, using your fingertips, press evenly until the ball is shaped into a round, flat disk. Gently lift the dough and stretch and rotate it until it is about 1/4 in/6 mm thick and 6 in/15 cm in diameter. Alternatively, using a rolling pin, gently roll out each ball into a round 6 in/15 cm in diameter. Try not to let the center of the disks become too thin in comparison to the edges. Gently lay the dough rounds on a lightly floured pizza peel or rimless baking sheet.

In a small bowl, stir together the mascarpone, 2 teaspoons sugar and egg yolks until evenly blended. Spread the mixture over the pizza rounds, dividing it evenly and leaving about 1 in/2.5 cm uncovered at the edges. Arrange the apple and pear slices attractively on the rounds, dividing evenly and overlapping the slices slightly. Sprinkle the rounds with the remaining 2 tablespoons sugar and the almonds. Quickly slide the pizzas onto the preheated stone, tile or baking sheet.

Bake until the edges of the dough are golden brown and the sugar is slightly caramelized, 15–18 minutes. Using a large metal spatula, remove the pizzas from the oven. Slide each pizza onto an individual dessert plate and serve immediately. Alternatively, transfer to a cutting board, cut each pizza in half and serve on individual serving plates.

Makes four 6-in/15-cm pizzas
Preparation/Cooking time
45 minutes

About Almonds

The sweet, creamy and delicious flavor of the almond is well known—and it may well be the most popularly eaten variety of nut. Certainly the diversity of the almond is well recognized. Almonds are included in savory dishes, such as Asian stir-fries, in salads and stuffings, and in sweet dishes such as biscuits and cakes, as well as nougat and marzipan. They can be eaten raw, roasted, slivered, ground and included in recipes as a paste.

Almond nuts are the seeds of the almond tree, which is native to south-west Asia. Today, almond trees are also widely grown in countries that surround the Mediterranean. In the United States, Californian groves of almond trees produce large annual crops of nuts. Some almond trees produce sweet nuts; others, bitter ones. Bitter almonds are not edible, though they are grown for their oil. Oil is also extracted from the sweet nuts.

Almonds contain more calcium than any other nut, and are rich in vitamin E. They also contain significant amounts of phosphorus and potassium. A large percentage of their fat is monounsaturated.

Pizza Tatin

The delicious flavor of these apples coated in caramel is not to be underestimated. Choose a sweet apple, such as Golden Delicious, rather than the usual Granny Smith. The effect of the orange juice in the pastry is an added flavor surprise.

INGREDIENTS

SWEET PIZZA DOUGH

1 cup/4 oz/125 g all-purpose (plain) flour*

1/2 tablespoon baking powder

1/8 cup/1 oz/30 g superfine (caster) sugar

4 tablespoons/2 oz/60 g butter

1/2 egg yolk

1/8 cup/1 fl oz/30 ml orange juice

TOPPING

4 whole/2 lb/1 kg Golden Delicious apples

1 3/4 oz/50 g butter

1/2 cup/3 1/2 oz/100 g superfine (caster) sugar

Cream, for serving

*1 cup/4 oz/125 g self-rising flour can be used instead of the all-purpose flour and baking powder

METHOD FOR MAKING PIZZA TATIN

Preheat the oven to 350°F/180°C/Gas Mark 4.

Place the flour, baking powder and sugar in a bowl. Rub in the butter. Add the egg yolk and enough of the orange juice to form a manageable dough, the consistency of pastry. (Alternatively, combine the mixture in a food processor.)

Wrap the dough in plastic wrap and chill in the refrigerator for 15 minutes.

Melt the butter in a 9-in/22-cm ovenproof frying pan. Add the sugar and cook over a medium heat, without stirring, to make a caramel, about 5–8 minutes.

Peel and quarter the apples and add to the pan. Cook gently for 3–4 minutes, tossing until coated with caramel. Arrange over the base of the pan.

Roll out the dough to fit the pan. Gently place the pastry on top of the apples. Bake in the preheated oven for 25 minutes, until golden.

Turn out onto a plate and serve hot, with cream.

Makes one 9-in/22-cm pizza
Preparation/Cooking time 1 hour 15 minutes

With this delicious pizza you can present the familiar flavors of old favorites—cooked apples for dessert and the delicious pastry-like base—in a new way.

About Apples

Apples, just like pizza, are a highly versatile food. They can be eaten raw or cooked, savory or sweet, be turned into a sauce or a juice—they can even be used to produce a devilish cider.

Apples have been a favorite fruit for millennia. They are the stuff of legends, from the Bible story of Adam and Eve to the adventures of William Tell. The charcoal remains of apples have been found in Stone Age ruins across Europe. The ancient Greeks grew apples, as did the ancient Romans, who took them to England and other parts of Europe. From England, the apple traveled to America with the colonists, though some settlers found that the Indians had already brought apple seeds from the East.

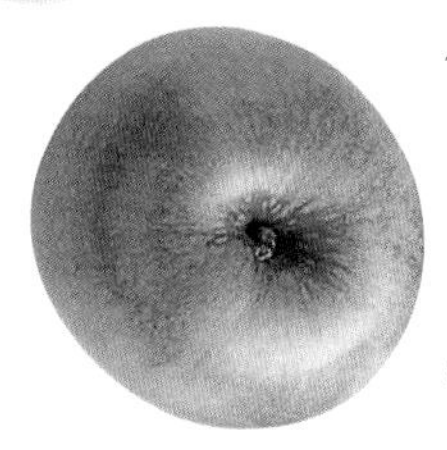

There are thousands of varieties of apples, yet grocers and supermarkets carry only the most profitable kinds. These include Red Delicious, Golden Delicious, Granny Smith, Fuji, Rome Beauty, Gravenstein, Starking and Jonathan apples. When choosing apples, select those that are mature, firm and smooth-skinned, with good color.

Berry Pizza

The "fruits of the forest", sweet and colorful berries are an alluring addition to any dessert. The types of berries you can choose for your topping include blackberries, blueberries, boysenberries, mulberries, raspberries and strawberries.

INGREDIENTS

2 quantities Sweet Pizza Dough (page 298)

8 oz/250 g mascarpone cheese

13 oz/410 g assorted berries, such as strawberries, blueberries and raspberries

METHOD FOR MAKING BERRY PIZZA

Preheat oven to 350°F/180°C/Gas Mark 4.

Roll out the dough into a 12-in/30-cm circle. Place on a buttered 12-in/30-cm pizza pan. Crimp the edges and bake for 20 minutes, or until golden. Cool and transfer to a serving platter.

Spread the mascarpone over the base. Top with the berries and serve.

Makes one 12-in/30-cm pizza
Preparation/Cooking time 1 hour 15 minutes

Sweet and creamy mascarpone cheese is here topped with the delicious flavors of fresh strawberries, raspberries and blueberries.

Orange Pizza

The biscuit- or scone-like base of this pizza provides the perfect foundation for the delicious sweetened cream cheese topped with segments of fresh oranges.

INGREDIENTS

BISCUIT (SCONE) DOUGH

1 1/4 cups/5 oz/155 g all-purpose (plain) flour*

1 tablespoon baking powder

1/8 cup/1 oz/30 g superfine (caster) sugar

About 1/3 cup/2 1/2 fl oz/80 ml milk

TOPPING

Zest (rind) of 1 orange, in julienne

1/2 cup/4 oz/125 g sugar

1/2 cup/4 fl oz/125 ml water

4 oranges

1/2 cup/4 oz/125 g cream cheese, at room temperature

Fresh mint sprigs, for decoration

*1 1/4 cups/5 oz/155 g self-rising flour can be used instead of the all-purpose flour and baking powder

METHOD FOR MAKING ORANGE PIZZA

Preheat oven to 350°F/ 180°C/Gas Mark 4.

Place the flour, baking powder and superfine (caster) sugar in a bowl and mix together. Add enough of the milk to form a manageable dough.

Roll out the dough into an 8-in/20-cm circle. Place on a buttered 8-in/20-cm pizza pan. Next prick the base all over with a fork, and then crimp or twist the edges of the pastry. Bake for 15 minutes, or until golden. Cool.

Place the orange zest (rind), sugar and water in a saucepan. Bring to the boil and simmer until the zest is softened, about 3 minutes. Drain and reserve the syrup.

Peel the oranges and remove all of the pith. Cut the oranges into segments, making sure to leave the membranes behind.

Beat together the cream cheese and reserved syrup until smooth. Spread the cheese over the cooled pizza base. Top with the orange segments and then the candied orange zest. Serve, garnished with mint.

Makes one 8-in/20 cm pizza
Preparation/Cooking time 1 hour

About Citrus Fruits

The widely popular—virtually indispensable—citrus fruits are a vital part of our diet, both for their flavor and for their high vitamin C content. Types of citrus include oranges, lemons, limes, grapefruits and mandarins. They are used to make snacks and juices and to add to the flavor of a wide variety of dishes.

Citrus trees are native to south-east Asia. They grow well in warm climates, and in the United States are grown in greater quantity than any other fruit.

Oranges are the most popular of citrus fruits. They are among the oldest cultivated citrus fruits, probably originating around India, Burma and south-west China. The modern sweet orange was first cultivated in the Mediterranean region, and is now grown throughout the world. Also highly popular, lemons originated in north-east India, near the Himalaya. They are now grown in the Mediterranean, as well as many other countries. Lemons are usually replaced with limes in more tropical areas.

Fruit Salad Pizza

Choose your favorite fruits to top this healthy and sumptuous pizza. The added dash of Cointreau liqueur gives it a delicious depth of flavor.

INGREDIENTS

2 quantities Biscuit (Scone) Dough (page 304)

4 oz/125 g ricotta cheese

1 tablespoon Cointreau or other orange liqueur

1 cup/8 oz/250 g fresh fruit salad, such as a mixture of kiwi fruit, banana, strawberries, star fruit, blueberries, grapes, mandarin, orange, cantaloupe (rockmelon), honeydew melon, pineapple and passionfruit pulp

METHOD FOR MAKING FRUIT SALAD PIZZA

Preheat oven to 350°F/180°C/Gas Mark 4.

Roll out the biscuit (scone) dough to fit a 12-in/30-cm buttered pizza pan. Prick the base all over with a fork and crimp the edges of the base with a fork.

Bake for 20 minutes, or until cooked and golden. Cool.

Combine the ricotta and Cointreau. Spread over the pizza base. Top with the fruit salad and serve.

Makes one 12-in/30 cm pizza
Preparation/Cooking time 1 hour

Tailor this pizza to your own preferences. Use a wide variety of fruits for their diverse tastes, textures and colors, or use only your most favorite fruits. Liqueur enhances the flavor; we've used Cointreau, but others will give equally tempting results.

Glossary

Here you'll find information about the various tools and ingredients used in this book.

ANCHOVY FILLETS

Caught in the waters that surround Italy, the tiny anchovy, a relative of the sardine, adds its intense, briny taste to pizzas and other dishes. Anchovies are commonly sold as canned fillets.

ARTICHOKES

Large flower buds of a variety of thistle, native to the Mediterranean. Also known as globe artichokes. When large, the tight cluster of tough, pointed leaves covers pale green leaves that form the heart.

ARUGULA

Also known as rocket, this green leaf vegetable has slender, multiple-lobed leaves and a peppery, slightly bitter flavor. Used raw in salads and panini and for topping pizzas.

BELL PEPPERS

Sweet, bell-shaped red, yellow or green peppers are also known as capsicums. Before use, peppers must have their seeds and pith removed. In Italy, red peppers are the most commonly used type.

bell pepper

CAPERS

The buds of a Mediterranean bush. A savory flavoring, they are most commonly pickled in salt and vinegar.

CHEESES

Among the most popular Italian cheeses used in this book are:
Fontina A creamy, delicate cow's milk cheese with a slightly nutty taste.
Goat Soft, fresh and creamy, goat's milk cheeses are notable for their mild tang.
Gorgonzola Dolcelatte A milder variety of the creamy, pale yellow, blue-veined cheese of Lombardy.
Mascarpone A thick, fresh cream cheese used to enrich sauces or desserts.
Mozzarella A mild, rindless white cheese, traditionally made from water buffalo's milk. Cow's milk mozzarella is firmer and is recommended for pizzas.
Parmesan This hard, thick-crusted cow's milk cheese has a sharp, salty flavor acquired during at least 2 years of aging. The finest variety is Parmigiano-Reggiano®.
Pecorino Sheep's milk cheese, sold fresh or aged. Among its popular aged forms is pecorino romano.
Provolone Cow's or water buffalo's milk cheese. Pale yellow, firm, with flavor ranging from mild to robust.
Ricotta A light, mild, soft fresh cheese. Originally made from sheep's milk, but cow's milk is now more commonly used.

Parmesan cheese

EGGPLANTS

Tender, mildly earthy, sweet vegetable–fruits covered with tough, shiny skin, which may be peeled or left on in grilled or long-cooked dishes. Eggplants vary in color from the familiar purple to white.

GARLIC

This intensely aromatic bulb has helped to define the character of Italian cooking since ancient times. To ensure the best flavor, buy whole heads of dry garlic, separating individual cloves from the head as needed.

HERBS

A wide variety of fresh and dried herbs add complex character to pizzas. Some popular varieties include:

Basil A sweet, spicy herb used both dried and fresh in pesto and tomato sauces and pizza toppings.

Oregano An herb with an aromatic, spicy flavor that intensifies with drying.

Parsley Although this herb is available in two varieties, Italian cooks prefer flat-leaf parsley.

Rosemary Used fresh or dried, strong-flavored rosemary frequently scents focaccia, poultry and lamb.

MORTADELLA

A specialty of Bologna, this wide, mottled pork sausage has a mildly spicy flavor and a fine texture that make it a suitable ingredient in pizza toppings.

MUSHROOMS

With their rich, earthy flavors and meaty textures, mushrooms are regularly featured on pizzas. Some types used in this book include:

Cremini Similar to common white mushrooms, they have a stronger flavor, a brown skin and tan flesh.

mushrooms

Shiitake Meaty in flavor and texture, these Asian mushrooms have large, flat, dark brown caps.
White These common cultivated mushrooms come in three sizes.

OLIVE OIL

Olive oil predominates in the cooking of Italy's warmer regions. Prized for its distinctive fruity flavor, extra-virgin olive oil is extracted from ripe black olives on the first pressing. Further pressings yield oil of lesser quality.

OLIVES

In Italy, particularly in the more southerly regions with harsher soil, olive trees thrive. Ripe black and underripe green olives are cured in combinations of salt, seasonings, brines, oils and herbs. Green olives may also be stuffed with pimientos, anchovies, tiny onions or almonds.

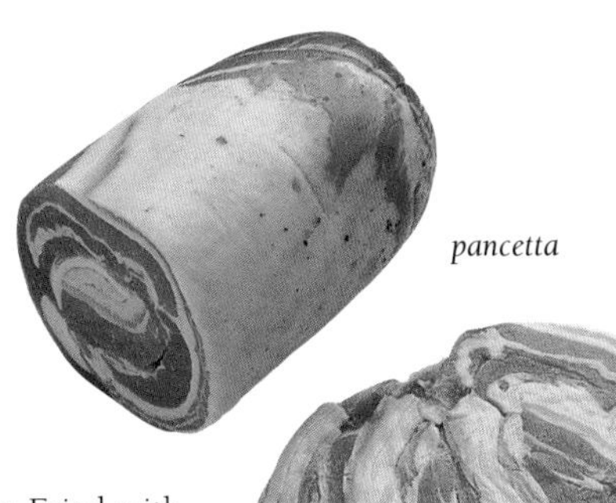

pancetta

PANCETTA

This unsmoked Italian bacon is cured simply with salt and pepper. Fried with onions and other vegetables, it forms the basis for many Italian dishes.

PIZZA PEEL

This is a wide wooden spatula with a long handle. It makes sliding a pizza into the oven a safe and simple task. If you prefer not to invest in a peel, you can use an inverted rimless baking sheet.

PROSCIUTTO

A specialty of Parma, a city in northern Italy, this raw ham is cured by dry-salting for 1 month, then air-drying in cool curing sheds for at least 6 months. It has a deep pink color and an intense flavor.

RADICCHIO

The most common variety of this type of chicory has small reddish purple leaves with creamy white ribs, formed into a oval. Also called red chicory, it has a rather bitter taste.

SALAMI

A type of cured, preserved sausage, usually made of pork but occasionally of beef, and often seasoned with herbs and spices. There are many different sizes and types of salami, with considerable variation between countries and regions.

salami

SAUSAGES

Sweet Italian pork sausages, popular in northern Italy, have a mild flavor and are sometimes seasoned with fennel seed or orange zest. Seek out, as well, the many innovative fresh sausages available today, including those made from chicken or duck, which may be substituted for sweet pork sausage.

SHALLOTS

These small cousins of the onion have a papery brown skin, purple-tinged flesh and a flavor resembling both sweet onion and garlic.

SHRIMP

Before cooking, fresh shrimp (prawns) are usually peeled and their thin, vein-like intestinal tracts removed. To peel and devein fresh shrimp, use your thumbs to split open the thin shell between the legs, then carefully peel it away. With a small, sharp knife, make a shallow slit along the back to expose the intestinal tract. Using the tip of the knife or your fingers, lift up and pull out the vein.

TOMATOES

Tomatoes were not popular in Italian kitchens until the 18th century. Today, they find their way into almost every course of a pizzeria meal, except dessert. The most familiar tomatoes, and those that offer the best quality year-round, are Italian plum tomatoes, also known as Roma or egg tomatoes. Canned whole plum tomatoes are the most reliable for cooking. At the peak of summer, also look for little cherry tomatoes and pear-shaped yellow tomatoes, which add intense sweet flavor and bright color to both salads and cooked dishes. Ripe tomatoes are also dried in the sun and preserved in olive oil or packaged dry.

ZUCCHINI

A squash native to the New World, the cylindrical green zucchini (courgette) long ago found its way into Italian kitchens. Use smaller squashes, which have a finer texture and tinier seeds than mature ones.

tomatoes

Index

Entries in *italics* indicate illustrations and photos.

E

F

G

H

M

O

P

Acknowledgments

Weldon Owen would like to thank the following people: Sarah Anderson, Lisa Boehm, Trudie Craig, Janine Flew, Peta Gorman, Michael Hann, Puddingburn Publishing Services (index)

Photography Ad-Libitum/Stuart Bowey, Kevin Candland, Rowan Fotheringham, Peter Johnson, Ashley Mackevicius, Joyce Oudkerk Pool, Chris Shorten, Weldon Trannies

Styling Janice Baker, Penny Farrell, Stephanie Greenleigh, Jane Hann, Susan Massey, Vicki Roberts-Russell, Suzie Smith